7/07

# CHILD SUPPORT MADE EASY

## Your Complete Guide to Collecting, Enforcing or Terminating the Court's Order

# CHILD SUPPORT MADE EASY

Your Complete Guide to
Collecting, Enforcing or
Terminating the Court's
Order

**Mary L. Boland**
*Attorney at Law*

SPHINX® PUBLISHING
AN IMPRINT OF SOURCEBOOKS, INC.®
NAPERVILLE, ILLINOIS
www.SphinxLegal.com

Second Edition: 2006

Published by: **Sphinx® Publishing, An Imprint of Sourcebooks, Inc.®**

Naperville Office
P.O. Box 4410
Naperville, Illinois 60567-4410
630-961-3900
Fax: 630-961-2168
www.sourcebooks.com
www.SphinxLegal.com

This publication is designed to provide accurate and authoritative information in regard to the subjec
matter covered. It is sold with the understanding that the publisher is not engaged in rendering lega
accounting, or other professional service. If legal advice or other expert assistance is required, th
services of a competent professional person should be sought.
*From a Declaration of Principles Jointly Adopted by a Committee of the*
*American Bar Association and a Committee of Publishers and Associations*

**This product is not a substitute for legal advice.**
*Disclaimer required by Texas statutes.*

## Library of Congress Cataloging-in-Publication Data

Boland, Mary L.
  Child support made easy : your complete guide to collecting, enforcing, or
terminating the court's order / by Mary L. Boland. -- 2nd ed.
      p. cm.
  Rev. ed. of: Child support : your complete guide to collecting, enforcing,
or terminating the court's order. 1st ed. 2004.
  Includes index.
  ISBN-13: 978-1-57248-571-6 (pbk. : alk. paper)
  ISBN-10: 1-57248-571-X (pbk. : alk. paper)
  1. Child support--Law and legislation--United States--Popular works.  I.
Boland, Mary L. Child support. II. Title.
KF549.Z9B65 2006
346.7301'72--dc22

                                                              2006026459

Printed and bound in the United States of America.
          SB  —  10  9  8  7  6  5  4  3  2  1

# CONTENTS

Change of Custody
Age of Majority of One Child
*Sample Petition for Modification of Child Support*

Adoption
Emancipation
Marriage of the Child
Service in the Military
Death of Paying Parent
Bankruptcy
*Sample Petition for Termination of Child Support*

Law Libraries
State Codes or Statutes
Case Reporters
Internet Research
Legal Encyclopedias
Digests
Form and Practice Manuals

Confidentiality
Finding a Lawyer
Initial Contact
First Interview
Fee Arrangements
Working with the Lawyer

# INTRODUCTION

According to the federal government, child support is the key to keeping millions of families from facing poverty. Yet, every year, several million custodial parents do not get the child support that has been ordered, and millions more do not even have child support orders. Unpaid child support now totals more than $107 billion.

About half of all children born today in the United States will live at some point in a single-parent family. According to the census figures released in July 2006, this translates into about fourteen million custodial parents in the United States. Even though the number of custodial fathers is increasing, mothers are the custodians in over 80% of cases. Nearly half of custodial moms have two or more children to care for, and even though more women work full-time, raising children is expensive. The poverty level for mothers with custody is much higher than it is for custodial fathers. Even with these factors, only about 64% of these mothers have child support orders.

In the late 1980s, the federal government and state laws began to make it easier to get and collect child support. Today, many parents work out their own agreements for child support and do not contact outside agencies for help. The most current figures show that over a million new child support orders were entered in fiscal year 2004 alone, and over $25 billion was collected. For these cases, less than half of the parents are paid the child support due to them. Another 30% collect only some of the money owed.

Who owes all this child support? Is it worth trying to collect it? While some parents cannot pay, others who reportedly make "no income" have money or assets that can be used to pay child support. In fact, of the accumulated past-due child support owed by the five million parents who have not paid, 63% show some income. Some parents settled lawsuits or collected federal benefits for themselves, such as Social Security and unemployment compensation, that could be used to pay child support. More than 160,000 parents who owed support had bank accounts with a reported value of $1 billion! So, it is certainly worth collecting your children's child support.

The goal of this book is to make you aware of your alternatives in attempting to get and collect on a child support order. You first learn what the law of child support is, how to establish parentage, and how to get a court order for child support. Enforcement is critical, and the alternatives to improve collecting on your order are covered next. The book also familiarizes you with what to do to modify your order and what to do when an order is terminated.

Finally, the book provides you with the resource information to enable you to file the necessary action to obtain and enforce your child support order. In the text, there are references to court cases that explain the principles of establishing parentage and child support. There are also references to statutes, such as the guidelines established by law in every state. To learn how to find these resources, refer to the section in the text on legal research. (see Chapter 11.) Each state's law on parentage and child support is included in Appendix B. A glossary of terms is also included.

# 1

# THE BASICS

Every parent—married or not—has a duty to pay for the support of his or her child. *Child support* is the legal obligation to support a child. It includes the child's basic living needs—such as housing, food, and clothing expenses—as well as medical costs and other expenses, such as education, after-school activities, and vacations.

Both parents share the responsibility to pay for the support of their child. This is true even if there was no marriage, if the noncustodial parent is not involved in the child's life, or if the parent is a minor when the child is born.

> **FOR EXAMPLE:** In one Illinois case, a father who was 15 years old at the time his child was born to his girlfriend argued that because he was a child himself, he should be protected from having to pay child support. The court rejected this argument, finding that the child's right to support outweighed the parent's right. *In re Parentage of J.S.*, 550 N.E.2d 257 (Ill. App.1990).

If the parents have married, the support obligation exists before, during, and after the marriage. The *Uniform Marriage and Divorce Act* permits either parent in a divorce or child support proceeding to be ordered to pay child support after consideration of all the relevant factors. Thus, it is a joint obligation. In some cases, even the parent who has full custody may be ordered to pay child support to the other parent while the child visits, because the decision of custody does not automatically answer the question of who should pay support.

In one unusual case, even a church was ordered to pay support. A husband and wife joined the church and turned over all their possessions to the church, expecting the church to support them. When the couple divorced, the father was ordered to pay support, but because all of his assets were given to the church, the Minnesota appellate court ordered the church to pay it.

## SUPPORT CANNOT BE WAIVED

The right to child support belongs to the child. That is why parents cannot negotiate away child support. An agreement not to seek support in exchange for termination of parental rights or an agreement not to seek custody or visitation will not be permitted. (*Swanson v. Swanson*, 580 S.E.2d 526 (Ga. 2003).)

One judge has observed that "people have the right to make 'bad deals,' but 'bad deals' do not extend to child support. The 'deal' was not simply an agreement affecting two independent parties. The most critical issue is the children's interests. Where such interests are compromised, courts must ensure that they are protected." (*Ordukaya v. Brown*, 814 A.2d 1138, 1145 (N.J. Super. 2003).)

However, once a parent secures a child support order and the amount of child support ordered becomes past due, it is considered a debt to the parent who already provided support. This is why past-due support (*arrearages*) can be subject to negotiation like any other debt, but current support must be paid until modified or terminated.

A parent cannot negotiate away the rights of his or her child to a reasonable level of support. So, a current support order is not subject to negotiation of the parents. For example, a parent cannot agree not to visit in return for a waiver of support. However, where one parent fails to pay child support, in effect, the other parent pays a double share. That past-due amount may be the subject of negotiation by the parents, because it is owed to the parent as reimbursement of expenditures.

## FACTORS CONSIDERED

Child support is determined by examining both parents' ability to pay and measuring the child's support requirements. Every state examines and weighs factors somewhat differently based on the legal child support guidelines in effect for that specific state. The guidelines are covered in more detail later in the book. You may also look in Appendix B for a summary of your state's specific factors for determining child support.

Of course, when parents come to an agreement on child support, they often agree on a support amount above the basic guidelines of their state law. This is because the guidelines are minimum threshold amounts, and parents who have the ability often agree that providing their child with a comfortable standard of living requires a support amount above what the guideline provides.

The amount of support is based on a number of factors, with the goal being to provide for the welfare of the child. Common factors include:
- financial resources of the child and parents;
- the physical and emotional condition of the child; and,
- the child's educational needs.

State guidelines also factor these items into their payment schedules.

**NOTE:** *Keep in mind that if the parents were married, misconduct during the marriage will generally not be considered in determining child support.*

## Financial Resources

Any child support order, to be enforceable, must take into account the ability of the parents to pay the amount due. Financial resources means more than just income. The parents' assets (bank accounts, property, etc.) and standards of living will also be considered. States' guidelines take into consideration the reasonable and necessary living expenses of a parent in determining a child support order.

## Needs of the Child

The needs of the child are perhaps the most prevailing factors for determining child support. State guidelines factor in a basic level of need. *Need* means more than just basic living requirements, but does not include unnecessary expenses.

If the parents have been married, a court may look at the standard of living the child had prior to the divorce or separation of the parents. If this is the case, the determination of child support will attempt to maintain that standard of living for the child.

## Health Insurance

Health care is a required element of all states' guidelines. If the parents do not agree to provide health insurance, a court will order it paid regardless of which parent has custody.

> **FOR EXAMPLE:** In Louisiana, in any child support case, the court may order one of the parties to enroll or maintain an insurable child in a health benefits plan, policy, or program.

In determining which parent should be required to enroll the child or to maintain such insurance on behalf of the child, the court considers each parent's individual, group, or employee health insurance program, employment history, personal income, and other resources. Unless agreed to by the parties, the determination of who pays health care premiums is made by the court or administrative agency, after consideration of such factors. The cost of health insurance premiums incurred on behalf of the child shall be added to the basic child support amount.

Other states provide for a health insurance coverage assignment. This means that a court order is entered that requires the noncustodial parent's employer (or other person providing health insurance to the noncustodial parent) to enroll the child in the parent's health insurance plan. The order also authorizes the employer of the noncustodial parent to deduct the cost of the health care premiums from the noncustodial parent's earnings.

States also provide for the award of extraordinary medical expenses where appropriate. In Kentucky, for example, this includes medical, surgical, dental, orthodontal, optometric, nursing, and hospital services.

## Education Expenses

The reasonable education expenses of a child may be agreed to, or the court may order one or both parents to pay for the education of a child. Some courts limit these expenses to public school education, but where the party has the ability to pay, a court may order payment for the cost of a private school and even a boarding school.

Although a college education may not be considered a *necessity* by some courts, if the parent has the ability to pay, the parties may agree to support a child after high school, through technical school or college. This often depends on the child's academic abilities and interests, and may require the child to maintain certain grade point averages. In most states, a court has the power to order the payment of educational expenses for a child if the parent has the ability to pay.

**NOTE:** *A 2004 New Hampshire law prohibits a court from ordering a parent to pay for expenses beyond high school in the absence of an agreement of the parties. (See N.H.R.S.A. 461-A:14.)*

## Other Expenses

Parents may also agree to or the court may order a parent to pay for various other expenses for a child, such as summer camps and vacation costs. One common item in the "other" category is child care costs for the time when a parent is completing his or her education or is job hunting. Many states' guidelines address this as an adjustment to the support obligation. In addition, all states' guidelines address extraordinary expenses and allow courts to make adjustments based on the best interests of the child.

## TAX CONSEQUENCES

Under current federal tax law, child support payments are neither deductible by the paying parent nor taxable to the receiving parent.

> **FOR EXAMPLE:** In Kansas, if the custodial parent does not share or alternate the income tax exemption, then a court will consider the effect of the failure to share the exemption on the noncustodial parent's monthly income, and may adjust child support accordingly. Since exemptions reduce taxable income, the value of the exemption to the noncustodial parent is calculated by multiplying the applicable exemption amount by the noncustodial parent's applicable highest tax rate at both the federal and Kansas levels. The combined federal and Kansas amount is then divided by 12 to arrive

at the monthly amount. A portion of this amount is then allocated to the noncustodial parent based upon his or her share of the combined income.

The tax law presumes that the parent with custody is entitled to take the tax exemption for the child. If the paying parent who does not have custody desires to take the deduction, the parent with custody must sign a form (Form 8332) or a similar statement agreeing not to claim the child's exemption. That agreement may cover one year, a number of years (such as alternate years), or all future years.

In some states, the federal and state income tax benefits of the parent who claims the federal *Child Dependency Exemption* are considered in making a child support award. Because the revenue rules do change periodically, check with your local Internal Revenue Service (IRS) office for the proper form and filing requirements. To find this information, go to **www.irs.gov** or look in the phone book under "Governmental Agencies" to find the address of the local IRS office.

## ELIGIBILITY FOR CHILD SUPPORT

Any parent or person who has custody of a child may be eligible to seek an order for child support. This includes grandparents, aunts, uncles, or any person who has custody of a child. Keep in mind, however, that when you file for child support, the other parent may sometimes counter with a request for custody or visitation. If this occurs, you should consult a lawyer.

## METHODS FOR FILING FOR CHILD SUPPORT

There are two methods of getting child support. You can file your own case, or you can seek assistance through the appropriate public agency designated to establish and collect child support in your state.

You can file an independent case to establish a child support order. In this case, parentage must also be established. Child support is also raised as an issue in divorce proceedings, custody actions, and parentage cases. In divorce proceedings, some states combine child support with support for a spouse into a *family support order*.

An application for child support enforcement services can be filed with a state agency through your local child support enforcement agency. A listing of agencies is included in Appendix A. In some states, you may also contact your local district attorney's office or your state attorney general. In this case, the agency will establish parentage, if necessary, with the support order.

## ROLE OF FEDERAL GOVERNMENT IN CHILD SUPPORT

The federal government has taken an active role in pursuing the collection of child support. Beginning in the 1970s and to this present day, Congress has passed numerous laws to improve the collection of child support.

The federal Office of Child Support Enforcement provides direction and guidance to state child support agencies, and funds various initiatives to improve local child support practices. Some of the major federal initiatives include the federal parent locator service (which matches information on parents who fail to pay with information collected by the Internal Revenue Service), the Social Security Administration, Veterans Affairs, the Department of Defense, and the Federal Bureau of Investigations. The federal case registry collects information on child support orders throughout the country. The national directory of new hires contains a list of all new employees in the country. Various federal laws permit tax refund intercepts and passport denials to parents who fail to pay. Finally, data matching with banking and financial institutions can also help to locate nonpaying parents. More information is provided on these and other programs that are being used by state agencies in Chapter 7.

The federal government also takes an active role in investigating and prosecuting some of the worst scofflaws. Its *Project Save Our Children* task force has been in existence for seven years and has federally prosecuted more than seven hundred persons, which has resulted in $21 million dollars of child support collected for families.

## ROLE OF CHILD SUPPORT AGENCIES

Any person, on public aid or not, can seek the services of a child support agency. Every state has a *child support enforcement program*, which is usually housed in the human services department or the state attorney general's office. Child support agencies help parents establish their legal rights to a child and set child support amounts. They do not usually assist in obtaining custody or visitation orders.

Although the program is open to any person entitled to a child support order, most often the program assists persons who have received public benefits through the *Temporary Assistance for Needy Families* (TANF) program, which was formerly called the *Aid to Families with Dependent Children* (AFDC). Under this program, public aid is paid to families and the recipients assign the right to collect child support to the government. If a family receives public assistance benefits and the parents are not married, the appropriate child support enforcement agency must establish legal parentage. The federal welfare law (*Personal Responsibility and Work Opportunities Reconciliation Act of 1996*) requires mothers to cooperate in establishing paternity in order to receive assistance.

Persons who are receiving public assistance, such as those on Medicaid or receiving TANF, are eligible to receive state support agency services for free. Many states charge a small fee for persons who are not receiving state aid.

> **FOR EXAMPLE:** Texas charges parents who receive more than $500 a year and have never received public assistance, but who use the state support enforcement agency services, an annual fee of $25. Texas also charges $10 for using parent locator services and $3 for case processing.

Some states do not charge for administrative filings, while others permit the fee to be paid over time. States also permit a parent to request a waiver of fees by filing a special request explaining why he or she cannot pay the fees and costs of maintaining the case.

It is important to remember that if you seek the assistance of an agency, the workers—including any attorney assigned to your case—work for the interests of the state, not you personally. There may also be a lengthy backlog of cases. See Appendix A for the listing of your state's child support enforcement agency. Also see Chapter 6 in this book for more information on working with your child support agency.

## DOMESTIC ABUSE

Many domestic violence victims are entitled to child support, but fear their safety in seeking it. In a series of studies done in Colorado of women seeking public assistance, 40% had a history of suffering domestic violence and 24% disclosed current abuse. Of the mothers reporting abuse by the fathers of their children: 81% reported being hit or beaten up; 69% faced threats of harm or death; 58% reported being isolated from their children; 57% reported being followed when attempting to leave; 44% reported being prevented from working; and, 34% reported being threatened with a weapon.

Some abused mothers change residences, move out of state, or stay in a battered women's shelter to escape their abuser. Abusers also threaten further violence, retaliatory custody claims, or child kidnapping to avoid paying child support.

In these cases, there is an exception that does not require the mother to assist in identifying the father of her child for purposes of public assistance benefits. Generally, the child support office will not attempt to establish paternity and collect support in those cases where the parent receiving public assistance is determined to have good cause for refusing to cooperate. This will enable the office to close the case.

The public assistance agency is required to provide public assistance applicants with written materials explaining their right to request a *good cause* exception. The public assistance agencies are listed in the phonebook under "Government Offices" or "Government Agencies," and most also have websites. For example, in Illinois, the Department of Public Aid administers the public assistance program. The good cause materials are often included with application forms and documents that explain requirements to cooperate with child support enforcement. The written explanations of good cause exceptions often include a list of the exceptions and the proof needed to establish an exception, such as medical records, police reports, or court orders.

> **FOR EXAMPLE:** In Minnesota, you do not have to cooperate if you can document that the establishment of paternity would result in physical or emotional harm to the child or physical or emotional harm to you that would reduce your ability to care for your child, or that the child was born as a result of incest or rape.

You need to file a written claim with the public assistance agency on a form provided by the commissioner of human services. After you file the written claim, you have twenty days to provide evidence of your claim. It is possible to get an extension of this twenty-day limit if the public agency believes you are trying to provide the evidence. You may request that the child support or public assistance agency help you to get the evidence.

If you have suffered domestic abuse, whether you seek the assistance of an agency or go through the process yourself, be sure to request confidentiality of your personal information to prevent it from being released to the abuser. Before you file any forms, check with the appropriate state agency for assistance in obtaining the necessary confidentiality documents.

# 2

# ESTABLISHING PARENTAGE

*Parentage* (the status of being a parent) must be legally recognized in order to obtain a child support order. Usually, identifying a mother is easy. When parents are married, if a child is born during the marriage, that child is presumed to be the child of the husband and wife. However, this is not the case when parents are not married. For the biological father to be considered the father under the law, he must establish *paternity* (fatherhood). Once paternity is established, a man becomes the legal father of that child, with the right to have or seek custody, visitation, or parenting time.

The child also gains certain rights. Having two legal parents allows the child to be eligible for medical care, Social Security, veterans' benefits, and inheritance rights from both parents. Children also benefit by knowing both parents' biological, cultural, and medical histories.

There are three basic ways that parentage can be established:
1. presumption;
2. acknowledgment; or,
3. judicial or administrative order.

## PRESUMPTION OF PARENTAGE

When parents are married, the mother and father are, by law, *presumed* to be the parents of the child. At the dissolution of the marriage, if the father attempts to challenge paternity, a court may not permit it.

> **FOR EXAMPLE:** In 1999, the Supreme Court of Connecticut did not allow the father to challenge paternity during the divorce proceedings. This father knew that the child was not his, but had treated the child as his own. The court found that since the man held himself out as the child's father during the marriage and since the child would suffer an emotional trauma if the father could now claim he was no longer responsible for her, the father could not change his mind. Also, in this case, the father had, by his actions, prevented the child from establishing a relationship with her biological father, who could not be located.

However, other courts have ruled differently.

> **FOR EXAMPLE:** In an Alaskan case, a husband was permitted to claim that the child born during the marriage was not his. In that case, the mother was already pregnant when the parties married, and the father was listed on the birth certificate and treated the child as his own for four years. The father then sought to reverse the determination of paternity and the court allowed it, even though the child was nine years old by that time.

Most courts require that the presumed father act promptly to make such a challenge.

The *Uniform Parentage Act*, which has been adopted by nearly half of the states, says that courts can presume paternity if the man openly treats the child as his and permits the child to live with him.

**FOR EXAMPLE:** In California, even if the parents are not married, paternity is presumed if the child lives with the father and the father openly treats the child as his natural child. In the case of *In re Nicholas H.*, 46 P.3d 932 (2002), the mother's live-in boyfriend was named on the birth certificate, even though he knew he was not the child's father. Still, the child was named after him and the parents lived together.

Eventually, the father sought custody due to the continuing nature of the mother's substance abuse problems. During the custody dispute, the Supreme Court of California determined that the presumption of fatherhood by conduct would stand.

## ACKNOWLEDGMENT OF PARENTAGE

If the parents have not married, all states have a process by which it is very easy to *acknowledge parentage*. The acknowledgment will be recognized in every state. When the child is born in a hospital or birthing center, the father can acknowledge paternity on the spot.

**FOR EXAMPLE:** In Pennsylvania, when the parents are not married, hospitals or birthing centers give parents the opportunity to acknowledge the paternity of the child by filling out a form at the child's birth. This form, called an *affidavit*, must be signed and witnessed by both parents.

States use different names for the forms used to acknowledge paternity. The form may be called an *Acknowledgment of Paternity* or a *Recognition of Parentage*. The parents are also provided with a written explanation of the parental duties and rights resulting from signing the form. The Social Security numbers and the addresses of both parents are included on the form. If the parents sign at the hospital, the father's name goes on the child's birth certificate and the mother does not need to go to court to prove paternity for the child. The parents get a copy and the hospital sends copies to the necessary state department, such as the Department of Public Welfare.

**NOTE:** *Be aware that the form may be a multipart document, so you may not be able to use a form that you have downloaded from the Internet.*

Parents who do not sign an acknowledgment of paternity at their child's birth can still sign the form at a child support enforcement office, local health department, or office that handles vital records, like birth records. If parents sign the declaration after the child's birth certificate has been issued, a new birth certificate can be issued with the father's name.

> **FOR EXAMPLE:** In California, if the parents do not sign the form in the hospital, the parents may sign and notarize the form, then mail it to the state Department of Social Services after the child's birth.

There will be a fee for adding the father's name to the birth certificate. However, it is important to have the birth certificate amended. For example, if a father later has custody of the child and tries to enroll the child in school, it becomes difficult when he has no birth certificate listing him as the father of the child.

If the father lives or moves out of state, paternity can still be acknowledged or determined by filing the necessary forms in your state and sending them to the father where he lives.

## Rescinding an Acknowledgment

There are instances in which a man acknowledges paternity, but later believes the child is not his. Many states provide procedures by which a man can cancel his acknowledgment of paternity. Some states have fairly short deadlines to do so. In some states, this cancellation can be done by completing a form and sending it to the proper agency. There may be a second form, sometimes called a *Rescission of Paternity*, that can be signed within thirty or sixty days. These forms are usually available at local child support offices, departments of vital statistics, and county clerks offices.

Some states require a father who has previously acknowledged paternity to file a case in court to get the matter resolved. This is the process suggested in the *Uniform Parentage Act* (2000) that a number of states have now adopted. Under the Act, if either the mother or father seeks to rescind an acknowledgment, a lawsuit must be filed and the case proceeds like a contested paternity case.

The father can also contest paternity later in a court proceeding, but it may be more difficult to do so. For example, some states allow a DNA test to be taken only until the child is 2 years old. In others, the case must be filed before the child reaches age 18.

> **FOR EXAMPLE:** In Minnesota, after sixty days, a court can vacate the *Recognition of Paternity* if there is proof that the document was fraudulent or signed under a mistake of fact, or the named father signed it under *duress* (coercion).

A court will *not* stay a child support order while the father attempts to contest his case.

**FOR EXAMPLE:** In a 1999 Ohio case, a child support agency sued a man who was named to be the father of a child in *Cuyahoga Support Enforcement Agency v. Guthrie*, 705 N.E.2d 318 (Ohio 1999). Mr. Guthrie did not answer the complaint, and a default judgment was entered against him finding that he was the father and ordering child support. Mr. Guthrie did not pay the child support, and he was threatened with having his tax refund intercepted and his delinquent amount reported to the credit bureau.

Mr. Guthrie then obtained a paternity test, which showed that he was not the biological father. The court then vacated the finding of paternity, but ultimately he was required to pay the *arrearage* that accrued before the order vacating paternity.

**FOR EXAMPLE:** In a similar decision, the Arkansas Supreme Court in *Littles v. Flemings*, 970 S.W.2d 259 (Ark. 1998) decided that where a DNA test thirteen years after the child's birth showed the father was not the biological father, paternity could not be vacated under that state's law, but future child support was vacated.

Some states treat this issue differently.

**FOR EXAMPLE:** The Maryland Supreme Court decided in *Walter v. Gunter*, 788 A.2d 609 (Md. 2002), that a man whose paternity is vacated cannot be held to pay thirteen years' worth of arrearages because the support order was invalid.

Recently, state laws have been passed allowing fathers a longer time to challenge paternity. For example, in Maryland, a statute permits a challenge to paternity regardless of when it was established. In Georgia, any man who has been ordered to pay child support can challenge his paternity and seek DNA tests. The view of such statutes is that the effect on the child of the father's challenge to paternity is irrelevant. In fact, one court has said that vacating an improper determination of paternity may provide some incentive to find the biological father.

In some states, mothers may also contest paternity.

> **FOR EXAMPLE:** In *In re Bruce*, 522 N.W.2d 67 (Iowa 1994), a mother decided to end her relationship with her longtime boyfriend, who had paid child support and treated the child as if it was his own. When the boyfriend sued for visitation, DNA tests showed he was not the biological father. The Iowa Supreme Court determined that the mother could keep her former boyfriend from having a relationship with her child.

An Illinois court has ruled differently.

> **FOR EXAMPLE:** In *Donath v. Buckley*, 744 N.E.2d 385 (Ill. App. 2001), a mother could not seek to vacate a paternity finding after she consented to having her boyfriend's paternity entered. Three years after the determination of paternity by consent, the mother decided to challenge paternity, and blood tests showed her boyfriend was not the biological father. Nonetheless, the court ruled that the case had to be filed within two years of knowledge of the true facts. Since the mother always knew that her boyfriend was not the father, she could not file the case.

## COURT ORDER OR FINDING OF PARENTAGE

If the father does not voluntarily acknowledge paternity and is not presumed to be the legal father, then the issue must be proven in court or to a hearing officer. Each state provides the requirements to establish that the person is the parent of the child. Regardless of whether the mother agrees, a man who believes he is the father of a child can also file his own case to establish paternity.

To establish parentage, you will need the name, date of birth, Social Security number, address, and phone number (if known) of the biological parent, as well as the child's birth certificate. Most states require that paternity be established by a *preponderance of the evidence*, meaning that paternity (or lack of paternity) is *more likely than not*. Putting this standard in terms of numbers, it means that there has to be a 51% weight to the evidence to find paternity. Some states insist on a higher, *clear and convincing* standard. This might translate loosely into a 75% weight of evidence, and is a tougher standard to meet than proving by a preponderance of the evidence.

## DNA TESTING

To establish parentage in a contested case, the father, mother, and child will usually be required to submit to DNA tests to prove maternity and paternity. Today, when paternity is at issue, DNA can provide results with tests of just the father and child. The results are highly accurate. With proper testing, most cases are decided on scientific evidence.

DNA testing includes either blood or swab collections from the individuals being tested. Depending on the test, either blood is drawn from the arm of each person or cotton swabs are rubbed against the inside of each person's cheek for cell collection. Most samples can be taken anytime after the child's birth. Test results usually take a few weeks. Home test kits are even available on the Internet for a few hundred dollars or less.

DNA is the genetic material in the cells of your body. At conception, every person receives half of his or her genetic material, or DNA, from the biological mother and the other half from the biological father. By comparing the DNA profiles of the mother, father, and child, one can determine the parents. DNA testing is very reliable (up to 99%) in determining whether a man is or is not the biological father. In most states, there is a presumption of paternity if the test results show a probability of paternity of 97% or higher.

The court can assess fees against the person who contests paternity, but will do so on an ability-to-pay basis. This includes the mother or putative father. If the test shows that the man is the father, he may be required to pay for the test fees, which may run $250–$400. If the test shows he is not the father, the court may waive or divide the costs between the parties. In cases filed by a child support agency, the agency usually pays the fee, but may seek to recover the costs later.

If the alleged father refuses to take a DNA test, paternity can still be established by applying the presumptions discussed above or by default. However, a court can order him to take the test or suffer contempt of court.

## WELFARE LAWS AND PATERNITY

The federal welfare law (*Personal Responsibility and Work Opportunities Reconciliation Act of 1996*) requires mothers to cooperate in establishing paternity in order to receive assistance. States require parents who receive assistance to cooperate in identifying and locating the parent of a child for whom aid is claimed. This means that parents may have to appear at their local child support office to provide information and documents. There is an application to complete for child support services. Some of the information requested about the noncustodial parent includes:

- name, date of birth, address, and Social Security number;
- name and address of current or recent employer;
- names of friends and relatives;
- names of groups or organizations to which he or she might belong;
- information about his or her income and assets, such as name and address of most recent employer, pay slips, tax returns, bank accounts, investments, or property holdings;
- physical description;
- child's birth certificate;
- if paternity is an issue, any written materials in which the alleged father has said or implied that the child is his;
- any current child support order; and,
- a marriage certificate, as well as any divorce or legal separation judgment or decree.

The custodial parent may also be required to appear at a hearing and provide testimony.

> **FOR EXAMPLE:** In California, the Department of Child Support Services opens a file and assign a caseworker to any custodial parent receiving assistance. Once a case is opened, a caseworker sends a letter to the custodial parent for an appointment as soon as the named father or mother is located. The caseworker explains the legal process to both parties. If the father has signed a *Voluntary Acknowledgment of Paternity* form, a petition to set support is prepared and filed with the court. If the father has not signed this form, a petition to establish parentage is set forth and filed with the court.

If the noncustodial parent requests genetic testing, the case is not set for court until the test results are received. If the named parent is found to be the biological parent, a court case is set to establish parentage and determine the amount of the support order, or the parties may enter into an agreed order. If the alleged parent is determined not to be the biological parent, the court action is dismissed. Where the alleged father is found not to be the legal parent, no support can be ordered.

# 3

# CALCULATING CHILD SUPPORT

Whether you are obtaining a child support order for the first time or reevaluating your current order to see if you qualify for a change, it is helpful to understand how child support is calculated.

All states have guidelines that help to determine the basic amount of support for a child. There is no single guideline model used in each state, but the states generally set forth their basic principles in their guidelines. It is important to note that the guidelines in each state are required to be reviewed at least every four years, so they may change periodically. Some courts provide computerized calculators that can determine the amount of support for your state.

> **FOR EXAMPLE:** In selected courthouses in California, the public can access computers in the courthouse that can calculate support based on the information entered.

If you are researching your state's guidelines, make sure you are using the most recent version of the guidelines. (See Appendix B for your state's law citations.) Application of the guidelines is presumed to result in the correct amount for a child support order.

Parents may agree to child support that is outside the guidelines. While parties may agree to deviations, any modifications must be reviewed prior to entry of a child support order, because the ultimate consideration is the *best interests of child*. Although adjustments can, and often are, made to the guideline amounts, generally a court (or administrative agency, if permitted) must make a written finding that the application of the guidelines would be unjust or inappropriate in a particular case.

Each state lists its own reasons for going above guidelines. They commonly include:
- child care expenses;
- medical and dental expenses (not already covered by insurance);
- educational needs (special school, tutoring, speech therapy);
- summer camp, sports teams, and after-school activities; and,
- additional income of the noncustodial parent.

Each state also includes reasons that a child support order may fall below guidelines. Common reasons include:
- shared or split custody of the children;
- extended parenting time arrangements;
- high cost of transportation for child visitation;
- high income of the noncustodial parent;
- the noncustodial parent's duty to support a second family;
- property division as part of a divorce; and,
- significant income of the child (such as from inheritance).

Each state lists the main principles of their guidelines. For example, California explains, in detailed fashion, the objectives of its guidelines.

> *In implementing the statewide uniform guideline, [California] courts shall adhere to the following principles:*

*(a) A parent's first and principal obligation is to support his other minor children according to the parent's circumstances and station in life.*

*(b) Both parents are mutually responsible for the support of their children.*

*(c) The guideline takes into account each parent's actual income and level of responsibility for the children.*

*(d) Each parent should pay for the support of the children according to his or her ability.*

*(e) The guideline seeks to place the interests of children as the state's top priority.*

*(f) Children should share in the standard of living of both parents. Child support may therefore appropriately improve the standard of living of the custodial household to improve the lives of the children.*

*(g) Child support orders in cases in which both parents have high levels of responsibility for the children should reflect the increased costs of raising the children in two homes and should minimize significant disparities in the children's living standards in the two homes.*

*(h) The financial needs of the children should be met through private financial resources as much as possible.*

*(i) It is presumed that a parent having primary physical responsibility for the children contributes a significant portion of available resources for the support of the children.*

*(j) The guideline seeks to encourage fair and efficient settlements of conflicts between parents and seeks to minimize the need for litigation.*

*(k) The guideline is intended to be presumptively correct in all cases, and only under special circumstances should child support orders fall below the child support mandated by the guideline formula.*
*(l) Child support orders must ensure that children actually receive fair, timely, and sufficient support reflecting the state's high standard of living and high costs of raising children compared to other states.*

Similarly, the Idaho guidelines state the same general principles, just a bit differently.

*A. Both parents share legal responsibility for supporting their child. That legal responsibility should be divided in portion to their Guidelines income, whether they be separated, divorced, remarried, or never married.*
*B. In any proceeding where child support is under consideration, child support shall be given priority over the needs of the parents or creditors in allocating family resources. Only after careful scrutiny should the court delay implementation of the Guidelines amount because of debt assumption.*
*C. Support shall be determined without regard to the gender of the custodial parent.*
*D. Rarely should the child support obligation be set at zero. If the monthly income of the paying parent is below $800.00, the Court should carefully review the incomes and living expenses to determine the maximum amount of support that can reasonably be ordered without denying a parent the means for self-support at a minimum subsistence level. There shall be a rebuttable presumption that a minimum amount of support is at least $50.00 per month per child.*

All of the states' guidelines assist in identifying minimum amounts to be paid for child support, and offer schedules of income and allowable expenses to calculate the presumed award amount. Even though the guidelines exist, each case is examined on its own merits, because no two families have exactly the same obligations and needs. The guidelines recognize this and make provisions for adjustments to the guideline amounts.

There are three child support guideline models that are used by the states. The *Income Shares Model* is the most popular. In this model, the parents' income is combined and then a proportion based on a formula is determined for child support. The following states follow this model.

- Alabama
- Arizona
- California
- Colorado
- Connecticut
- Florida
- Idaho
- Indiana
- Iowa
- Kansas
- Kentucky
- Louisiana
- Maine
- Maryland
- Michigan
- Minnesota
- Missouri
- Nebraska
- New Hampshire
- New Jersey
- New Mexico

- New York
- North Carolina
- Ohio
- Oklahoma
- Oregon
- Pennsylvania
- Rhode Island
- South Carolina
- South Dakota
- Tennessee
- Utah
- Vermont
- Virginia
- Washington
- West Virginia
- Wyoming

Most of the remaining states use a *Percentage of Income Model*. In this model, the state determines child support as a percentage of the noncustodial parent's income. This model presumes that the custodial parent pays support directly for the child. In some states, the model uses fixed percentages, but in others there is a sliding scale percentage to account for the lower and higher income levels. The following states use this model.

- Alaska
- Arkansas
- District of Columbia
- Georgia
- Illinois
- Massachusetts
- Mississippi
- Nevada
- North Dakota
- Texas
- Wisconsin

There is a third model, used by Delaware, Hawaii, and Montana, called the *Melson Model*. It is a more complicated version of the Income Shares Model. This model considers both parents' income and provides for a cost of living allowance. (For more information on this model, see *Dalton v. Clanton*, 559 A.2d 1197 (Del. 1989).)

## DEFINING INCOME

It is important to understand how income is defined in order to better comprehend the child support income models. The *income* used to determine child support may be *gross income* or *net income,* depending on your state's guidelines. Gross income will be defined by the guidelines and will usually include money, property, or services from most sources, whether or not it is reported or taxed under federal law. For example, exchanging services in return for goods without exchanging money will still be considered income, because the goods or services exchanged have a dollar or fair market value. This value is what is included as income. Income from public assistance programs is usually exempt.

> **FOR EXAMPLE:** Idaho's guidelines, which use the parents' gross income, define gross income as including income from any source, as well as, but not limited to, income from:
> - salaries;
> - wages;
> - commissions;
> - bonuses;
> - dividends;
> - pensions;
> - interest;
> - trust income;
> - annuities;
> - Social Security benefits;

- workers' compensation benefits;
- unemployment insurance benefits;
- disability insurance benefits;
- alimony;
- maintenance;
- any veterans' benefits received;
- education grants;
- scholarships;
- other financial aid;
- disability payments; and,
- retirement payments.

Idaho courts may consider when and for what duration the receipt of funds from other sources will be deemed as available for child support. These other sources include funds from:

- gifts;
- prizes;
- net proceeds from property sales;
- severance pay; and,
- judgments.

Unlike some states, in Idaho, benefits received by a parent from public assistance programs are included as gross income (except in cases of extraordinary hardship).

Recognizing that parents sometimes try to quit their jobs to avoid paying support, a court may use the parent's *earning capacity* rather than actual earnings to determine support. Earning capacity is commonly based on the parent's education, training, and work experience, and the availability of work in or near the parent's community.

Earning capacity is generally based on three factors:
1. ability to work;
2. willingness to work; and,
3. opportunity to work.

For ability to work, the court will examine factors such as age, education, health, work experience, and job qualifications. Willingness to work is normally determined by whether or not a parent has made a good-faith effort to work. Finally, the job market is examined to determine whether a parent will realistically find work. If the court looks at those three factors and determines that you should be earning money, it will base your child support order on what the court believes is your earning capacity.

> **FOR EXAMPLE:** A noncustodial parent voluntarily quits a job paying $40,000 a year and works part-time for $12,000. The court may use the earning capacity of $40,000, not the actual gross income of $12,000, to determine the amount of child support.

Some states' guidelines set out certain deductions from gross income to arrive at a net income figure from which the child support is determined. These deductions vary by type and amount permitted, but generally, standard deductions include:
- taxes;
- Social Security deductions;
- health insurance;
- mandatory retirement contributions; and,
- prior child support.

States may also permit subtractions from gross income for certain identified reasonable expenses. For example, income could be reduced because of business expenses that the court determines are reasonably necessary for producing income or operating a business.

## COMBINED INCOME MODEL

Many states' guidelines determine child support by combining the income of the parents, then calculating the guideline percentage of income available for support from each parent. This model is often called the *Income Shares Model*. The Indiana Child Support Guidelines uses this model, and explains that it is "based on the concept that the child should receive the same proportion of parental income that he or she would have received if the parents lived together."

Determining child support under this model generally involves five basic steps (although it may take several state worksheet pages to cover these steps).

1. Identify the gross and net income of each parent.
2. Add the income of each parent together for a combined total income.
3. Find the child support due for that total income amount on your state's guidelines.
4. Add or deduct the amounts that are permitted by your state.
5. Determine the proportionate share due from each parent based on the amount of income each contributes.

States that use this model recognize that the parent who has caretaking responsibilities pays the support directly for the child, while the other parent pays a dollar figure for child support.

> **FOR EXAMPLE:** To calculate child support for one child in Alabama, follow these steps.
> 1. Assume that the parent with custody has a gross income of $1,000 per month, while the noncustodial parent has a gross income of $2,000 per month.
> 2. The incomes are added: $3,000.
> 3. Next, look to the Alabama chart to determine the guideline formula.

| Combined Gross Income | 1 Child | 2 Children | 3 Children | 4 Children | 5 Children | 6 Children |
|---|---|---|---|---|---|---|
| 2900 | 426 | 660 | 826 | 931 | 1015 | 1085 |
| 2950 | 431 | 669 | 837 | 944 | 1029 | 1100 |
| **3000** | **437** | 677 | 848 | 956 | 1042 | 1114 |
| 3050 | 443 | 686 | 859 | 969 | 1056 | 1129 |

*(Alabama Child Support Schedule)*

The guideline provides for a child support sum of $437.

    4. For this example, assume no adjustments.

    5. Prorate the basic child support sum between the parents based on their income—the noncustodial parent will pay ⅔ ($2000/$3000) of the total due—**$291**.

**FOR EXAMPLE:** A similar result with the above example would be reached in Virginia. Once again, the parents' incomes would be added for a combined income of $3,000 (steps 1 and 2). Next, look at the guidelines in the Virginia law to determine the child support due (step 3).

| Combined Gross Income | 1 Child | 2 Children | 3 Children | 4 Children | 5 Children | 6 Children |
|---|---|---|---|---|---|---|
| 2850 | 430 | 667 | 836 | 941 | 1027 | 1098 |
| 2900 | 435 | 675 | 846 | 953 | 1039 | 1112 |
| 2950 | 440 | 683 | 856 | 964 | 1052 | 1125 |
| **3000** | **445** | 691 | 866 | 975 | 1064 | 1138 |
| 3050 | 443 | 686 | 859 | 969 | 1056 | 1126 |

*(Virginia Child Support Schedule)*

From the chart, the amount in Virginia would be $445. If there are certain allowable adjustments, such as a $50 expense for child care and $15 expense for extraordinary medical expenses, that would bring the total to **$510** (step 4). Now, under Virginia's scheme, prorate the amount due between the custodial parent and noncustodial parent (step 5). The noncustodial parent would pay child support under the Virginia guidelines of **$340**.

## PERCENTAGE OF INCOME MODEL

Another type of guideline commonly in use is based on the percentage of income of the noncustodial parent. Some states use a flat percentage, while in other states the percentage due under the guidelines depends on the level of income of the parent. As you will see from the examples, although the method of determining the child support is different, the result, if we use the same numbers, is not much different than previous examples in the last section.

Determining child support under this model generally involves three steps.

1. Identify the gross and net income of the parent who does not have custody.
2. Find in your state's guidelines the percentage of income due for child support.
3. Add or deduct any amounts that are permitted by your state.

The percentage of income guidelines in Wisconsin are typical.

> **FOR EXAMPLE:** Wisconsin law establishes that child support amounts are based on the belief that both parents are responsible for supporting their children, whether they live together or not. Therefore, this guideline

assumes that both parents will support their child. Although this type of guideline looks only at the income of the parent without custody, the guidelines again assume that the parent who has caretaking responsibilities will pay the support directly for the child, while the other parent will pay a dollar figure for child support.

Using the Wisconsin guidelines, apply the percentage from the guideline to the noncustodial parent's income. The percentages of the payment schedule in Wisconsin are as follows.

- 17% of gross income for one child
- 25% of gross income for two children
- 29% of gross income for three children
- 31% of gross income for four children

As reflected in the following chart illustration, if a noncustodial parent's gross monthly income was $1200, and there was one child, the support would be $204 (17%). If there were two children, the amount would increase to $300, or 25% of the gross income.

| Gross Monthly Income | 1 Child 17% | 2 Children 25% | 3 Children 29% | 4 Children 31% |
|---|---|---|---|---|
| $1200 | $204 | $300 | $348 | $372 |
| $2000 | $340 | $500 | $580 | $620 |

*(Wisconsin Child Support Schedule)*

To compare the guideline amounts with those in combined income guideline states, look at the earlier example of the noncustodial parent's income of $2,000. In Wisconsin, the chart shows that the guideline percentage for one child is 17%. Calculating 17% of $2,000 is

$340. Notice how this is very close to previous examples (Alabama and Virginia) of the combined income guidelines.

The point is that while states have different methods of reaching the basic support levels, they often lead to similar support amounts.

## ADJUSTMENTS

Many states permit add-on amounts or special adjustments. These may increase the basic support obligation or may reduce it. While each state has its own adjustment definitions, most include:

- extraordinary medical, psychological, dental, or educational expenses;
- independent income or assets of child;
- child support, alimony, or spousal maintenance previously ordered;
- age or special needs of child;
- split or shared custody arrangements; and,
- which parent takes the IRS dependency exemption.

States may also add other bases for adjusting child support orders. For example, in addition to the standard factors, some states allow a court to adjust child support based upon the following factors.

- The payment of support for a parent that has been paid regularly and for which there is a demonstrated need.
- Seasonal variations in one or both parents' incomes or expenses.
- The greater needs of older children.
- Special needs, such as costs that may be associated with the disability of a child, that have traditionally been met within the family budget even though the fulfilling of those needs will cause the support to exceed the proposed guidelines.
- The particular shared parental arrangement, such as when the children spend a substantial amount of their time with the secondary residential parent, thereby reducing the financial

expenditures incurred by the primary residential parent or the refusal of the secondary residential parent to become involved in the activities of the child or to give due consideration to the primary residential parent's homemaking services. If a child has visitation with a noncustodial parent for more than twenty-eight consecutive days, the court may reduce the amount of support paid to the custodial parent during the time of visitation not to exceed 50% of the amount awarded.

• When application of the child support guidelines requires a person to pay another person more than 55% of his or her gross income for a child support obligation for current support resulting from a single support order.

• Any other adjustment that is needed to achieve an equitable result, which may include, but not be limited to, a reasonable and necessary existing expense or debt. Such expense or debt may include, but is not limited to, a reasonable and necessary expense or debt that the parties jointly incurred during the marriage.

Courts must state the reasons for a departure from the guideline amounts.

> **FOR EXAMPLE:** In California, if the support order differs from the guidelines, a court must explain, in writing or on the record, the following information.
> • The amount of support that would have been ordered under the guideline formula.
> • The reasons the amount of support ordered differs from the guideline formula amount.
> • The reasons the amount of support ordered is consistent with the best interests of the children.

## PREEXISTING CHILD SUPPORT ORDER

One of the most common scenarios that affects the support guidelines is the obligations that remarriage and children bring. Even though there is a second family, it does not mean that the paying parent's responsibility to the first family ends. However, the amount of any future support order can be affected, because that parent does have the responsibility for supporting his or her other children.

In these cases, the guidelines may factor in as a deduction from income for the first child support order amount. For example, if the parent was obligated to pay monthly child support of $350 for a child born in 1990, and this parent's guideline income was $3,000 per month, the guidelines would subtract from income the first child's order amount ($3,000 less $350 = $2,650), then determine the support due using the new income figure for application to reach the second child's guideline amount in the current case.

> **FOR EXAMPLE:** In 2003, the Massachusetts Supreme Court ruled that child support orders cannot favor children born in marriage over those born outside of marriage. The case stemmed from a family court ruling that a doctor owed "primary" child support to his children born of the marriage and entered a lower order for the child he fathered outside the marriage. The court ruled that the guidelines applied equally to all his children.

## SHARED/JOINT CUSTODY

State guidelines deal with joint/shared custody arrangements in a number of ways. In some cases where the parents share nearly equal parenting time, the parents' *pro rata* share of support offsets each other so that they do not exchange support; they essentially pay all costs when the child is with them. In other cases, custody may be shared, but one parent spends more physical time with the child. In such cases, once again prorating the total amount due for child support, then factoring in the parenting time, will yield a sum to be paid for support.

Some states' guidelines include tables for adjusting the guideline amounts based on the percentage of shared parenting time.

> **FOR EXAMPLE:** If both parents were required to spend 17% of their income on their child, and Parent A had income of $2,000 per month and Parent B had income of $1,500 per month, then their initial child support due would be:
> Parent A—$2,000 x 17% = $340
> Parent B—$1,500 x 17% = $255
>
> However, if Parent A spends 44% (160/365 days) of the time with the child and Parent B spends the remaining 56% (205/365 days), then the state guideline schedule prorates the support due according to the following table.

| Percent of time with child | Percent of original child support amount |
|:---:|:---:|
| 43 | 56.71 |
| 44 | 53.38 |
| 45 | 50.05 |
| 46 | 46.72 |
| 47 | 43.39 |
| 48 | 40.06 |
| 49 | 36.73 |
| 50 | 33.40 |
| 51 | 30.07 |
| 52 | 26.74 |
| 53 | 23.41 |
| 54 | 20.08 |
| 55 | 16.75 |
| 56 | 13.42 |

Parent A owes 53.38% of the original total
($340 x 53.38% = $181.49)
Parent B owes 13.42% of the original total
($255 x 13.42% = $34.22)

Final calculations would show that $147.27 was due Parent B from Parent A ($181.49 - $34.22 = $147. 27).

This works out to a percentage due of 7.36%.

This is just one example of how state guidelines approach the shared parenting arrangement. Your state may treat this issue differently in its guidelines. Your local worksheets will help you calculate the proper amounts.

## SPLIT CUSTODY

States also attempt to apply their guidelines to cases in which the parents have more than one child and have sole custody of some, but not all their children.

> **FOR EXAMPLE:** If Parent A has custody of one of the three children, under state percentage of income guidelines, Parent A might pay 25% of his or her income as child support (for the other two children). Parent B would owe the guideline 17% for the one child in Parent A's custody.
>
> If their incomes are $3,000 for Parent A and $1,500 for Parent B, then support would be calculated as follows.
> Parent A: $3,000 x 25% = $750 (2 children)
> Parent B: $1,500 x 17% = $255 (1 child)
>
> Parent A owes Parent B the sum of $495 ($750 less $255 = $495) in child support.

## VISITATION

Visitation arrangements may result in an adjustment to a child support order. For example, some states prorate support based on time spent with each parent.

In Nebraska, the guidelines permit a reduction of 50% for visitation periods of four weeks or more. In addition, a court may adjust support due if visitation requires long-distance transportation costs.

# 4

# AGREEING TO CHILD SUPPORT

When parents can cooperate, decisions concerning child support can work to the benefit of all parties, especially the child. Recognizing this, most parents attempt to work out an agreement for child support. A court will consider the terms of an agreement concerning support, and if it is just and reasonable under your state's laws, the judge will award that amount. The amount and terms of your support agreement will then be included in your judgment.

If the court determines, however, that the amount is not fair or reasonable based on the laws of your state, then your agreement will not be binding on the court and the court may choose to make an award of child support that is different from what you have agreed to. For example, an agreement that in essence says *If you do not ask for visitation, I will not ask for child support* is unacceptable to the courts and will not be approved. Parties cannot prevent a court from making a reasonable child support order through their own bargaining process. In the case of *Lee v. Lee,* 699 N.W.2d 842 (N.D. S.Ct. 2005), the parties could not agree that the husband, as the primary guardian of the child, would pay reduced support to the wife in exchange for the wife not paying her share of the child support.

## FACTORS TO CONSIDER

In agreeing on a child support amount, the parents should consider a number of factors, including:

- what the state's guidelines require;
- additional quality of life or standard of living issues;
- each parent's financial resources;
- the needs of the child;
- who will be responsible for health care expenses;
- what educational expenses will be paid;
- other expenses;
- who takes the tax exemption;
- when and how payments will be made;
- whether there will be security (trust, life insurance) for the payments;
- what happens when the paying parent dies; and,
- if there is more than one child, what effect does it have on the payments if a child dies, reaches majority (age 18 or 21), marries, or joins the military.

## YOUR STATE'S GUIDELINES

In the previous chapter, you learned generally about the state child support guidelines in effect in every state. The guidelines that cover your case will be found either in your state's statutes, administrative rules, or court opinions. You can find the appropriate guidelines for your state by checking Appendix B for the listing for your state to obtain the legal citation. From your legal resource library, you can obtain the language of the guidelines. Many states also list their guidelines on the Internet, but be aware that these may not be the most current versions, since the guidelines are subject to review every four years. You can also contact your local child support enforcement agency for information on obtaining your state's guidelines.

Working through your state's guidelines may feel a bit like doing your taxes. Many states provide specific worksheets and forms to assist the process. These are available through your local clerk's office, local child support enforcement agency, and increasingly on the Internet.

With your state's guidelines as a basis, you can formulate an amount of child support to put into an agreement.

## DETERMINING YOUR BASIC GUIDELINE AMOUNT

Begin by determining your relevant income amount. Read your guidelines to determine whether your state is a combined income state. If so, begin by determining the amount of monthly income that both parents have. If your state is a percentage of income state, begin by determining the income of the parent without custody.

Look to your state's definition of *income* to see which amount (net or gross) the guideline is based on. For example, your state might include in its definition of *gross income*:
- salary, wages, interest, and dividends;
- commissions, allowances, overtime, or tips;
- business income;
- disability benefits;
- workers' or unemployment compensation;
- pension or retirement payments;
- Social Security benefits; and,
- maintenance, alimony, or spousal support.

Now look to your guidelines to determine which income amount (for both parents or just the noncustodial parent)—gross or net—will be applied to the formula for support of the number of children you have.

Next, if your state permits, deduct from your income the permitted amounts. If yours is a net income state, this will usually include:
- federal, state, and local income taxes;
- FICA;
- Medicare or self-employment taxes;
- mandatory union dues and retirement payments;
- health insurance (but not for the child);
- maintenance;
- alimony or spousal support paid; and,
- child support for other children.

## Total Your Income
In combined income states, you next add the final income amounts together for a combined total. In a percentage state, you only calculate the guideline amount from the paying parent (so do not combine incomes in those states).

## Add or Deduct the Permitted Amounts
Check your state's permitted adjustments to income to determine whether expenses can be added or deducted.

## Compare Your Income Amount to the Guideline
On the guideline schedule for your state, find the amount due for your income amount. In combined income states, determine the proportionate share due from each parent. In percentage states, find the percentage amount of income from the paying parent that will be due.

The *Sample Combined Income Child Support Worksheet* on page 49 will help you calculate support. In the percentage of income states, the *Sample Percentage of Income Child Support Worksheet* on page 50 will help you.

# SAMPLE COMBINED INCOME
# CHILD SUPPORT WORKSHEET

|  | Mother | Father | Combined |
|---|---|---|---|
| 1. Total Monthly Income: | _____ | _____ | _____ |
|     Less Monthly Deductions: |  |  |  |
|     Taxes | _____ | _____ |  |
|     FICA (Social Security) | _____ | _____ |  |
|     Health Insurance | _____ | _____ |  |
|     Mandatory Retirement | _____ | _____ |  |
|     Prior Child Support Order | _____ | _____ |  |
|     Total Deductions: | _____ | _____ |  |
| 2. Monthly Net Income: | _____ + | _____ = | _____ |
| 3. Line 2 x 12 (annual net): | _____ + | _____ = | _____ |
| 4. Now divide Line 2 for each parent by line 3's combined income sum: | _____ | _____ |  |
| 5. Find your state's Monthly Support Guideline Amount: | _____ |  |  |
| 6. Each parent's share: (Line 5 x Line 4) | _____ | _____ |  |

**NOTE:** *If your state uses the gross income method amount, carry that figure to line 2 without the deductions. Also, you may have other additions or deductions to income as permitted by your state.*

---

### SAMPLE PERCENTAGE OF
### INCOME CHILD SUPPORT WORKSHEET

Noncustodial Parent

1. Total Monthly Income: _____

2. Less Monthly Deductions:
   Taxes _____
   FICA (Social Security) _____
   Health Insurance _____
   Mandatory Retirement _____
   Prior Child Support Order _____

   Total Deductions: _____

3. Monthly Net Income: _____

4. Line 3 x 12 (annual net): _____

5. Line 4 x the percentage due
   under your states guidelines: _____

6. Line 5 ÷ 12 for
   the monthly support guideline amount: _____

---

**NOTE:** *If your state uses the gross income method, carry that figure to line 2 without the deductions. Also, you may have other additions or deductions to income permitted by your state.*

## DETERMINING YOUR CHILD SUPPORT AMOUNT

Now that you have determined the minimum guideline amount that would be acceptable in your state, you and the other parent should consider what additional amounts, if any, you believe would be best applied to your child's support.

Every year the federal government publishes an annual estimate of how much it costs for both parents who live together to raise a child. Using these figures, researchers have shown that on average, it costs around $7,000 every year to raise a child when the family income is around $40,000. When the family income is between $43,000 and $70,000, expenditures for raising a child increase to about $10,500. The figures increase in households with more than one child. Overall, housing accounts for the biggest share of the expense—about 35% of the total—followed by food (15%–20%) and then transportation (15%). (See U.S. Department of Agriculture Center for Nutrition Policy and Promotion, *Expenditures on Children by Families*: 2005 Annual Report.)

One researcher compared these expenditures to child support payments and found that the guideline amounts represented only about 20%–30% of raising a child. (See Mark Lino, *Do Child Support Awards Cover the Cost of Raising Children?* FAMILY ECONOMICS AND NUTRITION REVIEW, p. 29 (Winter, 1998).) This researcher's conclusion was that, overall, the guideline amounts were not adequate to raise a child. More recently, an economist compared state guidelines to 2004 estimates of child-rearing costs and found that twenty-two states had guidelines amounts that fell below the actual cost to raise one child. (See Jane C. Venohr and Tracy E. Griffith, *Child Support Guidelines: Issues and Reviews, 43 Fam. Ct. Rev.* 415, 422-23 (July 2005).)

Some states have raised their guideline amounts. You can compare your state's current guideline amounts to the United States Department of Agriculture annual expenditure amounts, or simply compute the cost of raising your own child on a monthly basis.

Check to see how it compares to the minimum guideline amount for a truer picture of how much you spend on child-related costs.

## WRITING THE CHILD SUPPORT AGREEMENT

Once you have worked through the relevant issues and determined that your agreement meets, exceeds, or is permitted to be less than the guideline amounts, begin writing. Make sure your written child support agreement covers:

- how much the payment shall be;
- the duration of the child support order;
- when and how child support will be paid;
- who is responsible for health care coverage;
- any special conditions of support; and,
- who will take the tax credit or exemption.

The agreement must indicate that the parents are fully aware of their obligations under their state's guidelines. For example, in California, a court will approve the parties' agreement for child support that is below the guidelines only if all the following are true.

- They are fully informed of their rights concerning child support.
- The order is being agreed to without coercion or duress.
- The agreement is in the best interests of the children involved.
- The needs of the children will be adequately met by the stipulated amount.

Language you might use to express a change from the guideline amount may be as follows.

> *Child support will be set in accordance with the State of _____ [your home state's] guidelines. We know this is the presumptively correct amount of the child support obligation. We know we can agree to pay more than the State guidelines require, and we also know that we cannot pay less without an approved reason under our state law.*

## Duration of the Order

The length of the child support order depends on the agreement of the parties or the terms ordered by the court. Many orders expire when the child reaches 18 years of age (the age of majority in most states), but parents may agree that they will support a child after he or she reaches the age of majority. This usually arises when the parents are in agreement that the child should go to college. Sometimes there will be an agreement to support the child until he or she becomes self-supporting.

Unless some kind of agreement is made beyond the period of time that a child reaches the age of majority, the court usually will not order such support. Sometimes, though, there is a state law that requires the parents to support their child longer. Some states extend support to age 19 if the child is still in high school. Maryland has a statute that permits a civil action to be filed when the child is *exceptional*, such as if the child has emotional problems. In Florida, a court held that parents of a disabled 50-year-old had a lifelong duty to support their dependent adult child. (*Hastings v. Hastings*, 841 So.2d 484 (Fla. App. 2003).)

An example of the language you can use to express the duration of the order follows.

> *We further agree that child support shall be paid until our child reaches the age of 18 (or 19 if still in high school), dies, marries, or joins the military. We also agree that we will review our child's progress and encourage our child to go on to college or technical school as his or her interests and abilities permit, and we agree to contribute sums towards our child's education beyond high school to the extent our financial situation reasonably permits.*

## Payments

Historically, the child support order required that payments be made directly to the other parent. However, this proved problematic and made enforcement very difficult. Some states still require payments made to the court clerk's office, but federal regulations implemented in the states now require a centralized location to process payments of child support, and most states have begun to implement this change.

> **FOR EXAMPLE:** In Nebraska, payments had been made to the clerk of the court, but that changed in 2004 when the state implemented a centralized payment center for the 100,000 payments processed every year.

More and more, payments can be made by credit card or even electronically over the Internet. In fact, some jurisdictions mandate that, unless the parties agree otherwise (and the court approves), the payments must be made to the state registry.

Many states have a form that must be filed with a child support order that provides information on the parents and child, so as to be able to properly track payments and disbursements through the state's central registry. Payment to the state registry allows a record of dates and amounts of payment to be kept. To be effective, of course, the parent entitled to payments must be sure to notify the registry if he or she moves. State laws require parents to keep registry information updated.

An agreement should include when and how child support will be paid. For example, the parents might agree to the following.

*Child support shall be paid by the paying parent on the 1ˢᵗ and 15ᵗʰ of every month to the state central registry for _____ [jurisdiction, county, or district].*

OR

*Child support shall be paid by the paying parent on the 1ˢᵗ
and 15ᵗʰ of every month to the receiving parent directly
beginning on _____ [date].*

Payment should begin under the order on the date of judgment.
However, a separate amount should be designated for support from
the date of filing of the petition. The parties should further agree to
the following.

*The paying parent agrees he or she is responsible to pay
child support from the date of filing of the petition to ____
(the date of the order) less the sum of $____ (the amount
already paid) as follows: $____ immediately and $____
on the 1ˢᵗ and 15ᵗʰ of every month.*

### Income Withholding

Automatic withholding of income (also called *wage withholding*) is
one of the simplest ways to pay child support. It is also one of the
most effective tools for collecting child support. Most often it takes
the form of a payroll deduction. If the paying parent is employed,
when the employer makes out the payroll, the child support is
withheld and sent to the clerk of the court in the county where the
court order was filed. The funds are then dispersed according to
state and federal laws. Certain fees may apply.

> **FOR EXAMPLE:** In Illinois, there is a clerk of court fee.
> Because the clerk of the court is the official record keeper
> for all child support payments, it is allowed to charge the
> noncustodial parent a $36 annual processing fee.

Income withholding is not limited to wages.

**FOR EXAMPLE:** Nebraska's income withholding law permits the withholding of nearly any kind of income, including:
- salaries/wages;
- unemployment and workers' compensation;
- investment funds; and,
- retirement plans.

In Washington, even inmates are subject to withholding.

### Electronic Funds Transfer

While some parents pay their child support directly by check, many states now offer an automatic payment option, known as *electronic funds transfer* (EFT). This automatically deducts the child support from your checking or savings account. This saves time preparing payments, saves money on postage and check fees, and ensures that your payments cannot get lost or delayed in the mail.

In Illinois, all employers with at least 250 employees must use EFT. Employers with fewer than 250 employees but with at least ten *Income Withholding Notices* must also use EFT to pay all child support amounts withheld (except for support orders entered in another state or those orders where the parties have agreed that payments not be made through income withholding).

### Receiving Child Support

Automated options also exist for receiving child support. If you are entitled to court-paid child support, you may be able to use a direct deposit method for your child support payments. Using direct deposit provides quicker access to the support funds, and your check cannot be delayed in the mail, lost, or stolen. In the states with an automated option, all that is needed is for you to have a checking or savings account, and the clerk of the court or the child support agency will electronically deposit your funds for you.

If the state agency is collecting and disbursing child support payments to you, it will most often use electronic funds transfer. Some states are also experimenting with debit cards—Iowa actually requires all disbursements to be paid this way. The custodial parent can use the card to make purchases or obtain money from ATMs. This helps parents who might not have a bank account, but also eliminates stolen checks, check cashing fees, and even hundreds of thousands of dollars of postage stamps.

## *Schedule of Payments*

Most states express child support payments as a fixed dollar figure. In the past, some child support orders were expressed as a percentage to allow the amount of child support to increase or decrease with the income level of the paying parent without the parties having to return to court. A combination order, for example—17% of gross earnings or $400 per month, whichever is greater—was intended to set a minimum amount of support while allowing the amount to increase with increased earnings. However, a percentage or combination order is harder to calculate, and therefore, more difficult to enforce.

Listing the child support obligation as a fixed dollar amount makes it easier to utilize orders for withholding. Also, a fixed amount allows past-due support to be automatically calculated and makes it easier to enforce an arrearage. Seasonal work hours can be adjusted in a fixed dollar amount, and there will be no need to recalculate when the paying parent quits a job or reduces working hours. Instead, the paying parent will have the responsibility to seek an appropriate modification. Keep in mind, however, that occasional overtime will not be factored into a fixed dollar amount unless overtime is consistent enough to be included in the order. Therefore, you should use a fixed dollar amount to schedule payments.

**FOR EXAMPLE:** Even though Wisconsin uses a percentage of income model to calculate child support, it requires all child support obligations to be expressed as a fixed monthly figure. This makes it easier for other states that require fixed dollar amounts to enforce Wisconsin's orders.

Check your state's guidelines for the appropriate method of stating the child support payment.

## Health Care

It should be clear in any agreement which parent is responsible for providing accident and health care coverage for the child. To make it clear, the parents might agree by using the following language.

*It is agreed that _____ (name) can obtain suitable health care coverage through an employer's group health plan at the most reasonable cost. Therefore, the parents agree that health, medical, dental, optical, and prescription drug care coverage shall be provided by _____ (the paying parent). The paying parent also agrees to increase insurance coverage if the child becomes eligible under the employer's group plan. For out-of-pocket health care costs above those covered by insurance, the parents agree to pro-rate the expenses according to our _____ (state) guideline percentage of support income, which is currently ___% for (Father) and ____% for ____ (Mother). These payments shall be made within thirty (30) days of the billing or insurance notice of payment due, whichever comes last. Both parties agree to promptly execute and deliver any necessary forms or documents to assure timely payment of insurance claims. The parties also agree that in the event the paying party fails to maintain insurance in violation of this provision, that party will be presumed to be responsible for all health care expenses incurred by the minor child.*

## Life Insurance

As security for future support, parents may agree to maintain life insurance on themselves, naming their child the beneficiary. In the agreement, parents might indicate this as follows.

*It is agreed that during the existence of the child support order for _____ (name of child), both parents will obtain and maintain suitable life insurance coverage in the amount of $_____ . Both parents further agree that their child _____ (name of child) will be named the irrevocable beneficiary of such policies. Each parent will provide the other with a copy of the policy and annual proof of payment of the premiums.*

## Tax Exemption

Parents should cover tax credits and exemptions in any agreement. For example, parents might agree to share the exemption, possibly passing it back and forth every other year. Typical language to this effect could read as follows.

*For income tax purposes, _____ (Mother) can claim _____ (Child) as an income tax exemption in odd-numbered years, and _____ (Father) can claim _____ (Child) as an income tax exemption in even-numbered years. Both parents agree to cooperate in the timely signing and filing of any required or necessary revenue forms to accomplish this purpose.*

# 5

# FILING
# FOR
# CHILD SUPPORT

There are certain basic steps to getting child support. Parents (or eligible custodians) may file for child support in their local courts, on their own or through an attorney. If you have worked out an agreement, you can include that agreement in your custody, visitation, or independent child support case.

If you handle your own case, you need to fill out, serve, and file several court forms. For example, a case to establish a child support order requires a complaint or petition to establish parentage (if necessary) and set support. A *Summons* is the form used to serve notice to the other party of the filing of the proceedings. There is also a financial affidavit or declaration form, and a child support worksheet that calculates your current income and deductions and applies the state's guideline schedule to determine the child support amount.

If the other party does not respond, the petitioner files a motion and order of default.

The other party may file a response to the petition. If paternity is an issue and is objected to, then the petitioner files a motion and order to require genetic tests. If the other party agrees to testing, there may be an order filed requiring a paternity test.

Unless paternity is acknowledged or stipulated to and a child support agreement reached between the parties, the case may next proceed to an administrative or court review, at which the parties' worksheets are reviewed and findings of fact are made on the petition and other documents filed in the case. Then, the hearing officer or judge will enter a *Judgment of Paternity* and *Order Establishing Child Support*.

Many courts and administrative agencies have developed forms for use by the parties in a child support case. If so, these forms may be mandatory. Check with your local clerk's office, child support enforcement agency, or online to see if a form exists for your jurisdiction.

Some states provide assistance to parents attempting to establish parentage and get child support orders.

> **FOR EXAMPLE:** In California, each county court provides free legal assistance to persons who cannot afford an attorney and are attempting to get child support. In addition, every county has an Office of the Family Law Facilitator to help fathers establish paternity and child support. Attorneys from this office help fill out the forms so that individuals can represent themselves. For fathers, these services include defense against paternity and child support actions, custody or visitation rights, and referral to other agencies, such as public assistance.

## TIME LIMIT FOR FILING

All states allow a case seeking to establish paternity and child support to be filed at least until the child reaches age 18. Either fathers or mothers can file the case. A child support enforcement agency may also file a case if the mother seeks public assistance for the child.

## FILING YOUR CASE

There are often several forms that must be filed with a complaint to establish paternity and child support. The petition will state your request for relief. States usually also require a child support worksheet or similar form, which may be called an *affidavit*, to be filed listing your expenses and income. Additional forms may be required in your state.

### Complaint

You will need some basic information for your *complaint*.

- You will need to list the name, address, and Social Security number of the biological parent to establish paternity.
- You will be required to state whether there are any previous actions regarding the child at issue.
- You will be required to state whether anyone else claims to have custody of your child.
- You may be required to state where the child has lived in the past few years.
- You may be required to state whether you have ever received public benefits for the child.

On the following page is a *Sample Petition for Paternity*. It is prepared with the mother being the *petitioner*, or the person bringing the claim. This basic form could be used if you are bringing an action on your own. Check with the court clerk's office to see if it has a specific form you are required to use.

# SAMPLE PETITION FOR PATERNITY
# AND CHILD SUPPORT

IN THE _____ COURT _____ , STATE

Petitioner,      )
v.             ) No. _____
Respondent.   )

## PETITION FOR PATERNITY AND CHILD SUPPORT

The Petitioner , _____ , states as follows:

1. I am the mother of and _____ is the father of _____ (name), _____ (DOB).
2. I reside at _____.
3. Respondent resides at _____.
4. The child has lived at the following addresses for the past 5 years: _____.
5. The child has lived with _____ in the past 5 years.
6. Petitioner has no knowledge of any other case concerning this child pending except: _____. (explain)
7. No other person claims to have custody of the child except: _____ _____. (explain)
8. No public assistance has been received for this child except: _____.

WHEREFORE, PETITIONER hereby requests this Court to:

A. Enter an order establishing that the parties are the parents of the child named in this petition.
B. Order genetic testing.
C. Determine the amount of any current and past-due child support and enter an order for payment of past support.
D. Allocate medical expenses for the child.

Dated: _____     Signature _____

## ACKNOWLEDGMENT

STATE OF _____ )ss
COUNTY OF _____ )
I,_____ , being first duly sworn upon my oath, depose and state that I am the Petitioner in the above-entitled cause. I have read the attached PETITION FOR PATERNITY AND CHILD SUPPORT. I state that the contents thereof are true and correct, except to the matters stated on information and belief, and those matters I believe to be true.

_____
Signature of Party

SUBSCRIBED AND SWORN TO before me on this day: _____.
My Commission Expires: _____.

_____
NOTARY PUBLIC

## Child Support Worksheet

Most states have child support information worksheets to follow in preparing for your child support case. Two examples of basic worksheets have been discussed earlier in this book. Check to see whether your state agency or local court has a particular form to use. When you have completed the necessary worksheets and other court or agency-required forms, you may file them and arrange for notice to the other parent.

# NOTICE

When taking a claim to court, you must know where the owing parent lives or works, so you can *serve* the other parent with the papers you filed. This notifies him or her of the filing of your case and allows the other parent to appear in court and answer the complaint.

Notifying the parent requires information on where the parent lives or works. If you do not know the current address or employer for the absent parent, the easiest way to find a person is through his or her Social Security number, although names and addresses of friends and relatives, past employers, banks, utility companies, clubs, and organizations may also prove to be helpful information.

*Service* must be made in accordance with state law. For example, in some states, service may be permitted by mail, sheriff's service, or acknowledgment. In certain circumstances, service may also be by publication in a certain newspaper.

The respondent (the other parent) can accept service and file a *response*. The local sheriff can serve the documents on the respondent. The notice may also be by publication when the respondent cannot be found, but this is not available in all states. States have forms for services, and the court or clerk's office can provide you with the necessary forms. In some states, the court notifies the noncustodial parent directly.

# SAMPLE CHILD SUPPORT WORKSHEET
### (Combined Income State)

Mother _____  Father _____

County_____  Case Number _____

**CHILDREN AND AGES:**

| **Part I: Basic Child Support Obligation** | **Father** | **Mother** |
|---|---|---|
| 1. Gross Monthly Income | $_____ | $_____ |
|   a. Wages and Salaries | $_____ | $_____ |
|   b. Interest and Dividend Income | $_____ | $_____ |
|   c. Business Income | $_____ | $_____ |
|   d. Spousal Maintenance Received | $_____ | $_____ |
|   e. Other Income | $_____ | $_____ |
|   f. Total Gross Monthly Income (add lines 1a through 1e) | $_____ | $_____ |
| 2. Monthly Deductions from Gross Income | | |
|   a. Income Taxes (Federal and State) | $_____ | $_____ |
|   b. FICA/Self-Employment Taxes | $_____ | $_____ |
|   c. State Employment Insurance Deductions | $_____ | $_____ |
|   d. Mandatory Union/Professional Dues | $_____ | $_____ |
|   e. Pension Plan Payments | $_____ | $_____ |
|   f. Spousal Maintenance Paid | $_____ | $_____ |
|   g. Ordinary Business Expenses | $_____ | $_____ |
|   h. Total Deductions from Gross Income (add lines 2a through 2g) | $_____ | $_____ |
| 3. Monthly Net Income (line 1f minus 2h) | $_____ | $_____ |
| 4. Combined Monthly Net Income (add parent's monthly net incomes from line 3) | $_____ | $_____ |
| 5. Basic Child Support Obligation (enter amount from state guidelines) | $_____ | $_____ |
| 6. Proportional Share of Income (each parent's net income from line 3 divided by line 4) | $_____ | $_____ |

**Part II: Health Care, Day Care, and Special Child Rearing Expenses**

7. Health Care Expenses
   a. Monthly Health Insurance Premiums Paid $_____  $_____
   b. Uninsured Monthly Health Care
      Expenses Paid                          $_____  $_____
   c. Total Monthly Health Care Expenses
      (line 7a plus line 7b)                 $_____  $_____
   d. Combined Monthly Health Care Expenses
      (add father's and mother's totals from
      line 7c)                               $_____  $_____
   e. Maximum Ordinary Monthly Health Care
      (multiply line 5 times .05)            $_____  $_____
   f. Extraordinary Monthly Health Care Expenses
      (line 7d minus line 7e, if "0" or enter "0") $_____  $_____

8. Day Care and Special Child Rearing Expenses
   a. Day Care Expenses                      $_____  $_____
   b. Education Expenses                      $_____  $_____
   c. Long Distance Transportation Expenses   $_____  $_____
   d. Other Special Expenses (describe)       $_____  $_____
   e. Total Day Care and Special Expenses
      (Add lines 8a through 8d)              $_____  $_____

9. Combined Monthly Total Day Care and
   Special Expenses (add father's and
   mother's expenses from line 8e)           $_____  $_____

10. Each Parent's Obligation for Special Expenses
    (multiply each number on line 6 by
    line 10)                                 $_____  $_____

**Part III: Gross Child Support Obligation**

11. Gross Child Support Obligation
    (line 5 plus line 10)                    $_____  $_____

**Part IV: Child Support Credits**

12. Child Support Credits
    a. Monthly Health Care Expenses Credit    $_____  $_____
    b. Day Care and Special Expenses Credit   $_____  $_____
    c. Other Ordinary Expenses Credit
       (describe)                            $_____  $_____
    d. Total Support Credits
       (add lines 12a through 12c)           $_____  $_____

**Part V: TOTAL CHILD SUPPORT**
       **OBLIGATION**           $_____   $_____

Other factors for consideration

_____

_____

**Signature and Dates**

I declare, under penalty of perjury, that the information contained in these Worksheets is complete, true, and correct.

_____

Mother's Signature                City and Date

_____

Father's Signature                 City and Date

## SAMPLE MOTION FOR PATERNITY TEST

IN THE _____ COURT _____ , STATE

Petitioner,        )
v.                 ) No. _____
Respondent.    )

### MOTION FOR PATERNITY TESTING

( ) Petitioner ( ) Respondent certifies that the following information is true:

1. I request that the Court enter an order for appropriate scientific testing of the biological samples of Petitioner and Respondent and the minor child(ren) listed below, so that a determination of paternity of the minor child(ren) can be made to a reasonable degree of medical certainty:

                  Name                       Birth Date

(1) _____     _____

(2) _____     _____

2. I request that the costs of the scientific testing initially be borne by ( ) Petitioner ( ) Respondent ( ) both Petitioner and Respondent.

I certify that a copy of this document was [check **one** only] ( ) mailed OR ( ) hand-delivered to the person(s) listed below on _____[date].

**( ) Petitioner ( ) Respondent**

Name: _____

Address: _____

City, State, Zip: _____

Dated: _____

Signature of Party: _____

Printed Name: _____

Address: _____

City, State, Zip: _____

Telephone Number: _____

## REQUEST TO ESTABLISH PATERNITY

Once the parent has been notified, paternity will be established if necessary. You may make a request for paternity testing using a form similar to the sample on page 69.

Once paternity is established, the next question is how much support should be awarded. (See Chapter 3 on calculating child support.) Answering this question requires the court to consider the financial information forms that must be filed in child support cases, and may require testimony from the parents and others, sometimes experts, regarding the contested income and expenses presented. In some cases, an administrative hearing officer decides the case, and the decision becomes an order if no party seeks a review by the court.

## TEMPORARY ORDER OF SUPPORT

Once the petition for support is filed, the case is set for an initial hearing. If the noncustodial parent is properly given notice of the proceedings, he or she must appear on that date and answer the petition. On this date, the court (or administrative agency, if permitted in your state) in which you file the application or petition for child support usually enters a *temporary order of child support*. Obtaining a temporary order of child support is made by a formal request to the court. The papers filed include the necessary worksheet information, and indicate the needs of the child or children. The temporary support amount should be payable immediately and continue until the court or agency officer has the opportunity to fully consider the documentation supporting the request for permanent child support.

## REQUEST TO DEVIATE FROM THE GUIDELINES

If you calculate that you will need more than what the guidelines provide for, you can ask a court to enter an order for child support in an amount that is higher than the guidelines. If you seek a reduced payment, you can file that request. In both cases, you need to provide an explanation that is permitted under state law for deviating from the guidelines. A *Sample Motion to Deviate from Child Support Guidelines* is on page 72.

# SAMPLE MOTION TO DEVIATE FROM CHILD SUPPORT GUIDELINES

IN THE _____ COURT _____ , STATE

Petitioner,      )
v.                      ) No. _____
Respondent.    )

## MOTION TO DEVIATE FROM CHILD SUPPORT GUIDELINES

( ) Petitioner ( ) Respondent requests that the Court enter an order granting the following: [check **one** only]

( )  MORE child support than the amount required by the child support guidelines. The Court should order MORE child support than the amount required by the child support guidelines because of:
[check **all** that apply to your situation]

    ( ) 1. Extraordinary medical, psychological, educational, or dental expenses;
    ( ) 2. Seasonal variations in one or both parent's income;
    ( ) 3. Age of the child;
    ( ) 4. Total available assets of mother, father, and child;
    ( ) 5. Impact of IRS dependency exemption and waiver of that exemption;
    ( ) 6. Any other adjustment that is needed to achieve an equitable result.

Explain any items marked above:

_____

( )  LESS child support than the amount required by the child support guidelines. The Court should order LESS child support than the amount required by the child support guidelines because of:
[check **all** that apply to your situation]

    ( ) 1. Extraordinary medical, psychological, educational, or dental expenses;
    ( ) 2. Independent income of child(ren), excluding the child(ren)'s SSI income;
    ( ) 3. Seasonal variations in one or both parent's income;
    ( ) 4. Age of the child;
    ( ) 5. The child spends a substantial amount of time with the noncustodial parent;
    ( ) 6. Visitation with nonresidential parent for more than _____ consecutive days;
    ( ) 7. Total available assets of obligee, obligor, and child(ren);
    ( ) 8. Impact of IRS dependency exemption and waiver of that exemption;
    ( ) 9. Child support guidelines require the obligor to pay more than __% of gross income for a support order; and/or,
    ( ) 10. Any other adjustment that is needed to achieve an equitable result.

Explain any items marked above:

_____

I certify that a copy of this document was [check **one** only] ( ) mailed or ( ) hand delivered to the person(s) listed below on _____ {*date*}.
Dated: _____ Signature of Party _____
Address: _____
City, State, Zip: _____
Telephone Number: _____

# SECURITY FOR PAYMENT

Where the parties have not agreed on a support amount, a court may order security for payment of a child support order. This may take the form of establishment or maintenance of a life insurance policy, or the creation of a trust for the children. Some states mandate that this be done.

Also, the court may order that the parent who pays support obtain a life insurance policy on him- or herself to protect the payment plan. In some states, a child support order may automatically create a lien on the paying parent's property. For example, the court could order a lien against the real estate of the parent who owes support, so that if support remained unpaid, the property could be sold to pay the lien.

A court can also order a parent to obtain required health care coverage through a special order called a *qualified medical child support order*. This requires that the employer's group health care plan provide coverage for a child. The employer can charge the parent for any premiums to carry out this order.

If the paying parent has a pension or retirement plan at work, the court can also order the employer to add the child on as a payee of the plan as security for the child support order, in what is called a *qualified domestic relations order*.

Many states use specific forms for child support orders, so be sure to cover all of your state's requirements. Check with your local court or clerk's office for a copy of the appropriate forms. A *Sample Child Support Order* form can be found on pages 74 to 77.

# SAMPLE CHILD SUPPORT ORDER

IN THE _____ COURT _____ , STATE

Petitioner,      )
v.           ) No. _____
Respondent.   )

## CHILD SUPPORT ORDER

The Petitioner having filed a petition, sworn to on_____,
_____ , alleging that the Respondent is chargeable with the support of [specify child(ren)]_____
and
[Check applicable box]:

( )  Respondent having appeared before this Court to answer the petition, having been advised by the Court of the right to counsel, and to show why an order of support and other relief prayed for in the petition should not be granted; and Respondent having ( ) denied ( ) admitted the allegations of the petition;

OR

( )  Respondent having failed to appear before this Court or to answer the petition after having been properly served; and

The matter having duly come on to be heard before this Court;

NOW, after examination and inquiry into the facts and circumstances of the case (and after hearing the proofs and testimony offered in relation thereto), the Court finds that:

1. The basic child support obligation for support of the following child(ren) is
   $_____
   <u>NAME</u>     <u>DATE OF BIRTH</u>     <u>SOCIAL SECURITY #</u>

2. The mother is the ( ) custodial ( ) noncustodial parent, whose pro rata share of the basic child support obligation is $_____
3. The father is the ( ) custodial ( ) noncustodial parent, whose pro rata share of the basic child obligation is $_____
4. The Court finds further that [check applicable box]:
     ( ) The noncustodial parent's pro rata share of the basic child support obligation is neither unjust nor inappropriate;
     ( ) Upon consideration of the following factors the noncustodial parent's pro rata share of the basic child support obligation is ( ) unjust ( ) inappropriate for the following reasons [specify]:
     The Court finds further that the parties have voluntarily stipulated to child support for the following child(ren) [specify]:
     payable by [specify]:_____to [specify]:_____
     in the amount of $_____ ( ) weekly ( ) every two weeks

The parties' reason(s) for agreeing to child support in an amount different from the basic child support obligation (is) (are) [specify]:

The Court approves the parties' agreement to deviate from the basic child support obligation for the following reasons:

5. The name, address, and telephone number of Respondent's current employer(s) are:
   NAME              ADDRESS          TELEPHONE

NOW, after examination and inquiry into the facts and circumstances of the case (and after hearing the proofs and testimony offered in relation thereto), it is ORDERED AND ADJUDGED that

A. the Respondent is chargeable with the support of the following person(s) and is possessed of sufficient means and able to earn such means to provide the payment of the sum $_____( ) weekly ( )every two weeks

| Name | Social Security # | Date of Birth | Amount | Per Time Period |
| --- | --- | --- | --- | --- |

B. the Respondent is responsible for the support from the date of the filing of the petition to the date of this Order (less the amount of $_____already paid) and that the Respondent pay the sum of $_____as follows:
   $_____ immediately, and $_____ ( ) weekly ( ) every two weeks;

C. the Respondent upon notice of this order, pay or cause the aforesaid amount(s) to be paid by ( ) cash ( ) check ( ) certified check ( ) money order to the: ( )Petitioner ( ) Central Child Support Collection Agency, such payments to commence on [specify]:_____;

D. An Order of Withholding be immediately enforceable and this Order shall be enforceable in any other manner provided by law;

E. The Court having determined that [check applicable box]:
   ( ) The child(ren) are currently covered by the following health insurance plan [specify]:_____ which is maintained by [specify party]:_____
   ( ) Health insurance coverage would be available to one of the parents or a legally-responsible relative [specify name]:_____ under the following health insurance plan [specify, if known]:_____,
   which provides the following health insurance benefits [specify extent and type of benefits, if known, including any medical, dental, optical, prescription drug, and health care services, or other health care benefits]:_____
   ( ) Health insurance coverage is available to both of the parents as follows:
   Name    Health Insurance Plan    Premium or Contribution  Benefits

IT IS THEREFORE ORDERED that:

( ) _____ continue to maintain health insurance coverage for the following eligible dependent(s) [specify]:_____ under the above-named existing plan for as long as it remains available;

( ) _____ enroll the following eligible dependent(s):_____ under the following health insurance plan [specify]:_____ immediately and without regard to seasonal enrollment restrictions, effective as of [specify date]: _____, _____, and maintain such coverage as long as it remains available in accordance with the Qualified Medical Child Support Order.

**OR**

( ) This Court having found that neither of the parties have health insurance coverage available to cover the child(ren), it is hereby ORDERED that the custodial parent [specify name]: shall immediately apply to enroll the eligible child(ren) in the _____ (state health insurance program for children).

And the Court further finds that:

The mother is the ( ) custodial ( )noncustodial parent, whose pro rata share of the cost or premiums to obtain or maintain such health insurance coverage is_____,

The father is the ( ) custodial ( ) noncustodial parent, whose pro rata share of the cost or premiums to obtain or maintain such health insurance coverage is_____;

And the Court further finds that [check applicable box]:

( ) Each parent shall pay the cost of premiums or family contribution in the same proportion as each of their incomes are to the combined parental income as cited above;

**OR**

( ) Upon consideration of the following factors [specify]: _____ prorating the payment would be unjust or inappropriate for the following reasons [specify]: _____ and, therefore, the payments shall be allocated as follows [specify]: _____ _____

The legally responsible party immediately notify the other party of any change in health insurance benefits, including any termination of benefits, change in the health insurance benefit carrier or premium, or extent and availability of existing or new benefits; [specify name]:_____ shall execute and deliver to [specify name]:_____ any forms, documents, or instruments to assure timely payment of any health insurance claim for the child(ren); Willful failure to obtain health insurance benefits in violation of this order will result in liability for all health care expenses incurred on behalf of the above-named dependent(s) from the first date such dependent(s) ( ) was ( ) were eligible to be enrolled to receive health insurance benefits after the issuance of such order or execution directing the acquisition of such coverage; Additional pro rata share of future reasonable health expenses of the child(ren) not covered by insurance shall be paid by _____ as [check applicable box]: ( ) direct payments to the health care provider ( ) other [specify]: _____;

If health insurance benefits for the above-named child(ren) not available at the present time become available in the future to the respondent/petitioner, such party shall enroll the dependent(s) who are eligible for such benefits immediately and without regard to seasonal enrollment restrictions and shall maintain such benefits so long as they remain available.

F.  ( ) The noncustodial parent herein, pay the sum of $_____ ( ) his ( ) her pro-portionate share of reasonable child-care expenses, to be paid as follows:

_____

_____

G.  ( ) The noncustodial parent herein, pay the sum of $_____

as educational expenses by ( ) direct payment to the educational provider ( ) other [specify] _____

H. ( ) The petitioner/respondent check applicable box(es): ( ) purchase and maintain ( ) life and/or ( ) accident insurance policy in the amount of [specify]: and/or ( ) maintain the following existing ( ) life and/or ( ) accident insurance policy in the amount of [specify]:_____ and/or ( ) assign the following as ( ) ben-eficiary ( ) beneficiaries [specify]:_____to the following existing ( ) life and/or ( ) accident insurance policy or policies [specify policy or policies and amount(s)]: _____

In the case of life insurance, the following shall be designated as irrevocable benefici-aries [specify]:_____ during the following time period [specify]:

_____

In the case of accident insurance, the insured party shall be designated as irrevocable beneficiary during the following time period [specify]:_____

The obligation to provide such insurance shall cease upon the termination of the duty of [specify party]: _____to provide support for each child.

ENTER

_____

Judge or Hearing Officer

Dated: _____

Check applicable box:
( ) Order mailed on [specify date)s) and to whom mailed]:_____
( ) Order received in court on [specify date(s) and to whom given]:_____

## RESPONDING TO A PETITION FOR CHILD SUPPORT

When you are served with a petition seeking child support, you may deny paternity, admit paternity, challenge the amount of support sought, or agree to pay the support.

### Statute of Limitations

If you wish to deny paternity, check to make sure the petition was filed within the allowable time frame. Most states have *statutes of limitations* that govern the period within which a case may be filed. Many states require paternity to be established by the child's age of majority, which is usually 18 years old. Some states permit paternity to be established within two or three years of the date that the child reached the age of majority. If the case to establish paternity is timely, many states permit an order of support to date back to the child's birth. Others place limits on how far back a child support order can reach.

> **FOR EXAMPLE:** In Maine, a support order can reach back as far as six years from the date of filing the case. However, in Iowa, as long as the paternity case is filed within the proper statutory period, the order of support can reach back to the child's date of birth.

Some states also establish limits on what kind of support can be retroactive.

**NOTE**: *Check to be sure that the petition covers an eligible child.*

### Paternity

Paternity may be raised as a defense against a request for child support. To be ordered to pay child support, you must be found to be the father of the child in question. If you question whether you are the father, you can deny the allegation and your case will be scheduled for a DNA test. If the test determines that you are not the father, the case will be dismissed. If the test shows that you are the father, the court will enter a judgment of paternity and an order of child support. You can also file a claim for custody, visitation, and/or child support along with your answer.

## Provide Financial Information

You may wish to challenge the child support amount requested on the grounds that it is the product of incorrect income basis, adjustments, or expense items. States' guideline amounts may be adjusted upward or downward based on a number of factors. If you agree that child support is due your child, you will answer the petition and provide your own financial affidavit. The court will review it so that a complete picture of the child's needs and the parents' resources can be evaluated, and a proper child support award can be determined.

**NOTE:** *Be aware, however, that failure to obtain the agreed upon (or ordered) visitation is not a defense to avoid paying child support.*

It is also important to be aware that once a child support order is entered by a court, it must be paid in money. Gifts of clothing and other items instead of money will not be credited against the support amount due, unless a court gives the parent prior permission to do so.

## Default

Ignoring a complaint for child support does not prevent the entry of a *judgment of support.* All states require the defendant (who may also be called a *respondent*) to respond within a certain time limit to the notice of the child support petition. For example, the *summons* may require that an *answer* (or response) be filed within thirty days.

If the defendant fails to respond, he or she can be *defaulted.* This means that the case proceeds without the defendant present. The court can legally determine that the defendant is the mother or father and is responsible for paying child support, and can impose other costs of the proceeding on the defaulting parent.

A parent can challenge a default judgment if the parent was not properly notified of the court case. The parent has to prove that he or she did not get served with the complaint and *summons,* and acted promptly to set aside the judgment when he or she learned of the case.

Perhaps the biggest danger in failing to respond to a complaint for child support is that the court in a default judgment case will rely on the state's child support guideline amounts. Also, the parent who filed the petition will be able to introduce evidence of additional need, and the support amount may accordingly be higher than the guidelines. The support amount may not reflect your ability to pay. Nonetheless, past due support is not able to be modified. Avoiding the case can make your situation much worse.

# 6

# WORKING WITH YOUR LOCAL CHILD SUPPORT ENFORCEMENT AGENCY

Every state has a child support enforcement agency. These programs are designed to improve the self-sufficiency of families through increased financial and medical support, and to establish paternity for children born outside of marriage. Some states allow these programs to establish paternity and child support administratively, which is faster than going to court. The administrative order is just as binding as one entered in court.

The names and addresses of each state's agency appears in Appendix A. Every state agency provides some basic services, including:
- establishing paternity (fatherhood);
- finding parents;
- establishing and enforcing child support orders;
- modifying child support orders; and,
- collecting and distributing child support payments.

Most programs do not provide the following services:
- divorce;
- custody/visitation;
- protective orders; and,
- spousal support orders.

If you are in need of other services beyond those provided by the child support agency (such as divorce or aid assistance), referrals may be available through the agency, as many agencies have formed partnerships with private service providers in the local community.

## OPENING A CASE

Any parent who needs to establish or modify a child support order (or paternity) can use the services of a child support agency. If you are not receiving public assistance, there may be a small fee for services, as well as other fees that may be deducted from payments you receive (or make).

To open a case with a child support agency, you must visit the proper local agency. (See Appendix B for your state's information.) Be prepared to complete certain paperwork to provide information about yourself, the other parent, and your children.

### What Should You Bring?

Every agency has its own forms (check Appendix B to find your state's website to see if checklists or forms are available online). All will require at least the following information.

About you and the other parent:
- names;
- addresses;
- dates of birth;
- Social Security numbers;

- recent picture of other parent;
- employer names, addresses, occupations;
- income information, such as tax returns for the past two years;
- marriage license and divorce documents, if any; and,
- any additional information that will help to locate the other parent, such as the names and addresses of family, friends, clubs, associations, and past employers.

About each child:
- name (and address if the child does not live with you);
- birth certificate;
- child's Social Security number;
- any special needs or expenses;
- proof of paternity (even letters or notes from a father may help if there is no official proof);
- any support previously paid; and,
- any prior child support order.

## CASE MANAGEMENT

Your case will be assigned a caseworker, who will then use the enforcement tools available to find the other parent and notify him or her that legal action may be taken to obtain an order for support.

For example, your local child support enforcement agency may have resources that can assist in finding the absent parent. State child support enforcement agencies have *State Parent Locator Service* (SPLS) facilities that can help find the absent parent. The SPLS will use the parent's Social Security number to check records of other agencies within your state, such as the motor vehicle registration, unemployment insurance, and income tax agencies, as well as prison or jail facilities in an effort to find the absent parent. They can also request information from utility companies, schools, employers, and post offices.

Even so, it may be one to six months before the necessary procedures are undertaken and an order of support entered. This period can be longer if the other parent lives out of state or there is a backlog of cases.

### Application of the Guidelines

The agency uses the state's child support guidelines to calculate the amount of support due. All orders entered through a child support agency have a provision for health care coverage for the child (such as including the child on an employer's policy, or paying directly for health insurance or health care bills).

## INCOME WITHHOLDING

All child support orders entered through a child support agency must have immediate income withholding, unless both parents agree to an alternative arrangement. See Chapter 7 for more information and a sample order for withholding. If an immediate withholding order is entered, usually a one-month arrearage automatically triggers the withholding order. The employer must then treat the order like any other payroll deduction. If the parent does not have an employer, some agencies use automatic billing, telephone reminders, and delinquent notices, in addition to other enforcement tools, to achieve payment.

All wage withholding orders are paid directly to the state child support agencies. Child support agencies are required by law to promptly distribute child support payments collected.

## PERIODIC REVIEW

Child support agencies will review child support orders at least every three years, or if there is a significant change of circumstances (upon request of a parent). Some states do this automatically.

For many parents, obtaining the child support order is just the first step to collecting support. The biggest challenge is actually collecting the support due. While some parents no doubt pay all the child support ordered on time, many do not. Some move to other states, and even though they have ample resources, feel that they should not have to pay. This is why the federal government stepped in and provided new enforcement options. These laws serve to make enforcement easier within the same state and to make laws uniform for parents who live in different states.

In 1996, strong new tools and penalties were added and states began implementing strict child support enforcement techniques. In 2003, Alabama child support collections reached $256 million, North Carolina collected nearly $536 million, and Florida collected almost $1 billion!

Several states have formed partnerships with private companies to increase child support collection.

## "MOST WANTED DEADBEATS"

Some states have begun holding press conferences and developing press releases on the state's worst *deadbeat parents*. One of the newest methods that is creating a lot of attention on parents who refuse to support their children is the posting of *Wanted Posters* on the Internet, naming the top several deadbeat parents who owe large amounts of child support. These strategies have received some strong responses from the parents listed.

> **FOR EXAMPLE:** In Massachusetts, more than $1.3 million has been collected in overdue child support since the first *Most Wanted* poster was created in April 1992.

When Connecticut posted its fourth poster on the Internet, three of the parents turned themselves in to begin a payment plan. These three parents reportedly owed a combined total of more than $110,000 in back-due support.

Illinois launched a *Most Wanted* website in November 2003 and promptly collected $37,000.

In a new twist on the *Most Wanted* idea, Arizona, in the summer of 2003, launched a *Deck of Deadbeats* and posted an online deck of cards featuring names and faces of delinquent parents.

In 2000, Alabama began permitting state newspapers and the website of the Department of Human Resources to list the names and pictures of ten parents from any county who have been delinquent on their child support payments and ask the public for help in locating these parents. The delinquent parents get notice prior to publication and can stop the printing of their name and picture if they:

• make a child support payment of at least the monthly amount required by the support order or a percentage of the overdue and unpaid child support payments, whichever amount is greater;
• give their current address;
• provide verification from their current employers of their wages, salary, and compensation; and,
• provide verification that a withholding of their wages, salary, or other compensation has been arranged in order to pay the child support payments and the delinquent payments.

On the federal level, the U.S. Postal Service is working with states to display wanted lists of parents who owe child support in post offices.

Each state can provide its to the Postal Service, and the list will be displayed in post offices within that state.

## OUT-OF-STATE PARENTS

About 30% of parents who owe past-due child support do not live in the same state as their children. As you might expect, the most difficult child support cases are those in which a parent who has been ordered to pay child support lives in one state, and the child and the custodial parent live in another. All states provide methods to get child support in these cases.

Relatively new methods of tracking parents are making it easier to find absent parents and enforce delinquent orders. In the 1990s, the federal Office of Child Support Enforcement undertook a pilot program to track down these delinquent debtors. In a short period of time, over 60,000 delinquent parents had been located under a matching program conducted by certain states.

This led to new federal laws in 1996 that established a federal *Case Registry and National Directory of New Hires* to track delinquent parents across state lines. Employers are now required to report all new hires to state agencies, which in turn report new hire information to the National Directory. This program is very effective. In the first six months of operation, the National Directory found over 90,000 delinquent parents who owed child support.

> **FOR EXAMPLE:** In Idaho, one of the top ten deadbeat parents was arrested as a result of the New Hire Registry. This parent left Massachusetts and moved several times to evade investigators, allegedly owing more than $45,000 in back child support. Eventually, he moved to Idaho, where he got a job with a state university. A routine reporting of new hire data collected from Idaho

employers and sent to the National Directory in Washington, D.C. matched information against the federal Case Registry, a database that holds child support cases from all fifty states. This parent was arrested on *fugitive from justice* charges and was held to answer to why he did not pay child support.

Under a federal law called the *Uniform Interstate Family Support Act* (UIFSA), state enforcement agencies are required to cooperate with each other in handling requests for assistance. All states have adopted UIFSA laws substantially similar to the federal model and rely on these laws in seeking enforcement in other states. The UIFSA provides extended powers to states to reach beyond their own state lines to establish support orders. All states have a *Central Registry* to receive incoming interstate child support cases, review them to make sure that the information given is complete, distribute them to the right local office, and reply to status inquiries from child support offices in other states. The information in this registry is then sent regularly to the federal registry for matching with new hires and other reported financial and residency information.

**NOTE:** *Be prepared—it can take several months for a custodial parent to receive support from an out-of-state parent.*

## PARENT LOCATOR SYSTEMS

Part of the 1996 welfare reform law mandated the development of what has come to be known as the *Federal Parent Locator Service* (FPLS). The FPLS was intended to coordinate communication between certain federal and state agencies with employers and financial institutions. Parts of the system were called the federal Case Registry, National Directory of New Hires, Federal (tax) Offset Program, Passport Denial Program, and Financial Institution Data Match. By late 1999, these programs were brought together and the

FPLS was implemented. Now a database can be accessed to provide information about new hires, tax refunds, passport applications, bank accounts, wages, and employment insurance to match against active child support cases. These agencies have access to:

- birth, death, and other vital statistics records;
- federal and state tax files;
- real estate records;
- motor vehicle records, including car title information;
- occupational licenses;
- recreational licenses;
- business licenses;
- unemployment records;
- public assistance information;
- police and law enforcement records;
- public utility billing information; and,
- cable companies.

The child support agencies can even subpoena credit card information or put a boot on a delinquent parent's car. For example, Virginia's booting program has brought in more than $65 million.

If the absent parent has moved out of state, the state can ask the FPLS for assistance. The FPLS will search the records of the Internal Revenue Service (IRS), Social Security Administration, Department of Veterans Affairs, and state Employment Security Agencies (among others) for a current address or employment information on the absent parent. The FPLS can also find the duty station of any payor in the military.

When a delinquent payor is in the same state as the child, the State Parent Locator Service (SPLS) can use the same methods to check the state agency records. In January 2004, Kentucky launched a new automated system that feeds past-due child support cases into its Department of Revenue to make it easier to seize bank accounts,

wages, and tax refunds, and to place liens against homes and prop-
erties of deadbeats. The process works by first warning the parent
that he or she has twenty days to make a good-faith effort to pay. If he
or she fails to do so, the case is turned over to the revenue department.

> **FOR EXAMPLE:** Ohio has a program that places a freeze on
> the sale or refinance of a home if the homeowner
> matches the state parent registry for delinquent child
> support. Implemented in the fall of 2003, the program
> immediately began to get results. In one case, a man
> was required to pay $25,000 before he could sell his
> two houses.

If you are pursuing your own collection efforts, you can still request
assistance from the child support agency in finding the parent. There
is usually an application and small fee for this limited parent locator
service, and it may take several months to complete the agency inves-
tigation. You will be asked to provide as much information about the
absent parent as possible, including his or her name, Social Security
number, date of birth, address, parents' and friends' names and
addresses, past employer information, and any other information you
might have that can help locate the absent parent.

## INSURANCE SETTLEMENTS

A new method of collection is done by intercepting insurance claim
settlements. Around 4% of insurance claimants owe delinquent child
support. Several states so far have joined together in a Child Support
Lien Network to pool delinquent child support cases into a database
that matches the information to insurance settlements. The Child
Support Lien Network was originally developed by Rhode Island,
and has expanded to include Arkansas, California, Connecticut,
Florida, Illinois, Iowa, Maine, Missouri, New Hampshire, New Jersey,
New Mexico, Oklahoma, Pennsylvania, Rhode Island, South Dakota,

Tennessee, Texas, Vermont, Virginia, and West Virginia. Once a match is found, the insurance company notifies the appropriate state and a lien is filed against the proceeds. The network estimates that $2 billion of personal injury and workers' compensation claims can be redirected to delinquent child support orders. For example, in the first six months after Iowa joined the Network, it matched active open insurance claims in fifty-six cases and obtained $8.8 million in payments from insurance settlements.

## FINANCIAL INSTITUTION DATA MATCH

The *Financial Institution Data Match* program was developed as a result of welfare reforms in 1996. The laws required banks and other financial institutions to agree to provide information on accounts to be compared with child support records. Every state has such a program. This program seeks to discover hidden bank accounts belonging to parents who are delinquent in paying their child support. Before this program, delinquent payors put their funds in undiscovered bank accounts. Even if the parent or agency owed support found the account, it required notice to the parent and a judge's order to seize the account. By then, the money was gone. Now, once a computer identifies the account, it is immediately frozen if the delinquent payor meets certain criteria. Every state can determine the specific factors that must be present to initiate a seizure.

> **FOR EXAMPLE:** In South Carolina, the payor must owe at least $1,000 or be six months behind. The delinquent parent has ten days to dispute the seizure or the money is paid to the arrearage.

## DENIAL OR LOSS OF LICENSE

Part of the child support enforcement reforms that have gone into effect permit states to suspend or deny applications for driver's licenses or professional licenses. This is a very effective tool to ask a court to use in enforcing a child support order. *Deadbeats Don't Drive* is the nickname of a series of laws passed in an effort to make parents catch up on overdue child support. In the 1990s, a few states authorized restrictions on licenses where parents refused to pay their child support orders. In the late 1990s, as another part of the welfare reform laws, all states were required to begin the process of passing laws restricting or suspending licenses for failure to pay child support. Today, all states have a version of these laws in place.

> **FOR EXAMPLE:** In Illinois, the typical deadbeat is about eight months late in making payments and owes around $1,500. The financial responsibility law applies to parents who are three or more months behind. The judge notifies the secretary of state's office that he or she has held a parent in contempt for failure to pay child support, and the driver is then notified that he or she has sixty days to pay or have his or her license suspended. The court can order a hardship permit for travel to work or for medical purposes during the period of suspension. Most parents pay up rather than losing their licenses.

Nebraska's law permits the state to suspend the driver's, recreational, and professional licenses of parents who owe more than three months support. To avoid suspension, the parent must be in compliance with a payment plan for the payment of the past-due support.

In Mississippi, the license suspension law applies to all regulated occupations and professions, from barbers to social workers to physicians, and extends to those seeking business and liquor licenses, as well as driver's licenses and hunting or fishing licenses. Mississippi has a database that links the license information against those who are at least two months behind in their payments. Once notified, if the delinquent parent fails to work out a payment plan, the licensing agency suspends the license. A suspended license may be reinstated if the delinquent parent subsequently pays or agrees to a payment plan. These sanctions are very effective.

> **FOR EXAMPLE:** In Connecticut, in less than a year's time, the threat of losing a license has led to $12 million dollars in payments of past-due child support. Between August 2003 and January 2004, Tennessee sent about 20,000 delinquent parents, who owed at least $500 in support and were overdue for more than ninety days, notices that their licenses were subject to revocation. This resulted in 7,000 license revocations, but the state still collected $5 million in overdue support.

It is also important to note that your state may permit this sanction even after the child reaches the age of majority if past-due support is still outstanding.

> **FOR EXAMPLE:** In Montana, a father's driver's license (along with his electrician's license) was suspended based on his child support delinquency, even though the children had been emancipated. (See *In re Hopper*, 991 P.2d 960 (1999).)

## LOSS OF TAX REFUND

Since the early 1980s, the U.S. Department of Treasury has been intercepting tax refunds to collect delinquent child support. All states participate in this program. By 1995, the federal government estimated that over $1 billion in refunds had been intercepted for 1.2 million families. The federal government is very aggressive in this program—by 1996, refunds intercepted were up 66% since 1992.

In 2004 alone, nearly 1.4 million families benefited from the $1.5 billion in past-due child support collected from tax refund intercept programs. The average amount collected was $1,104.

Today, federal financial assistance can be denied, and civil service retirement payments and federal salary payments can be intercepted to pay overdue child support. This allowed $1.64 billion to be intercepted in 2001, with approximately $264 million in the form of the tax rebates. Today, even lottery winnings of a parent may be subject to interception and applied to overdue child support.

> **FOR EXAMPLE:** In Louisiana, racetracks and casinos are authorized to intercept winnings over $1,200 if the parent is delinquent on child support.

Tax refund interception is possible today because most states now have computer database systems that record child support due and payments for that state. This is another reason why it is useful to have payments made through the clerk of the court. Once a year, the states report the names of parents who owe overdue child support to the Internal Revenue Service and to their state's department of revenue. These federal and state agencies in turn deduct the past-due amounts and pay them to the state child support account for payment to the parent owed the support.

Now, adult children who are owed past-due child support can use the tax refund interception program. There are threshold amounts that must be overdue for eligibility in the program.

**FOR EXAMPLE:** Currently in Wisconsin, the past-due amount must be $500 for the federal program, but only $150 for the state refund intercept program. Be aware that there may also be a small processing fee taken out of the refund paid to the state. In Wisconsin, the fee will not be more than $25, and no fee is due if the refund is not paid.

To protect against inevitable mistakes, before any refunds are intercepted, a notice will be sent to the paying parent's last known address, explaining the program and how he or she can appeal. If the amount sent to the state is more than the amount owed at the time the tax refund is received, the extra sum will be refunded to the tax-paying parent.

There are a number of limitations on tax intercept efforts. For example, no matter how much overdue support is owed, the *most* that can be intercepted is the amount of the refund. Also, only the amount submitted will be intercepted.

Also, to minimize repayment of an amount intercepted, amounts intercepted from a federal joint tax return are held for up to six months before getting passed on to the parent owed the support. Even this does not guarantee that money received will not be recalled by the IRS or the state department of revenue, because tax returns can be amended for up to six years.

For more information about your state's tax refund interception program, find your state's child support agency information in Appendix B.

## CONSUMER CREDIT BUREAU REPORTING

If a parent owes a considerable amount of past-due child support, he or she can be reported to the consumer credit bureaus that track credit records. Having a child support debt on a credit record can mean not being able to get a loan or a new credit card.

## LIENS AND SEIZURE OF PROPERTY

A state may permit liens against any real property of the payor parent in that state. In some states, all child support judgments are automatic liens on the parent's real property, such as his or her house. The lien keeps the parent who owes child support from selling or refinancing the property until all the past-due child support is paid.

A parent may seek to seize and sell the property of a parent who owes a substantial amount of past-due child support. If the parent who owes past-due support has bank accounts or investments, those assets are sometimes taken to pay back child support through a process called *garnishment*. The federal *Consumer Credit Protection Act* limits the amount of wages that may be withheld to 60% of disposable wages. The percentage increases if the delinquency is longer than twelve weeks. State law varies and may further limit the amount available for garnishment.

## PASSPORTS

Another enforcement tool that can be used to assist in collecting child support is denying approval for a passport. Under federal regulations, passport applications can be denied if the noncustodial parent owes $2,500 or more in overdue child support.

**FOR EXAMPLE:** In November 2003, child support officials worked together in Michigan and California to nab a parent who lived in an affluent suburb of Los Angeles by denying the renewal of his passport due to a large arrearage. The parent, who needed to do business overseas, reportedly paid $289,542.

Over $12.5 million was collected as a result of this program in the first nine months of 2005. In many cases, collection of large lump sum amounts come from the denial of a passport for a parent who secures employment overseas. Collections are expected to continue to increase since passports are now needed to travel to and from Canada, Mexico, Central and South America, the Caribbean, and Bermuda.

## CONTEMPT

Historically, using *contempt of court* proceedings was the most commonly used enforcement method for parents who had the ability to pay but refused to do so. Once a court found the parent in contempt of court, he or she might be sent to jail for nonpayment of child support and permitted to get out of jail only by paying the contempt (or a scheduled) amount. Today, this power is combined with a number of the other options, such as license suspension.

To avoid being held in contempt for failure to pay support, you must show that you did not have notice of the order, you could not pay the order, or that your failure to pay was not willful. However, spending your income to support a new girlfriend or boyfriend will not be excused. Quitting a job or intentionally taking a lower-paying job is also not an excuse for nonpayment.

## CRIMINAL PROSECUTION

The threat of criminal prosecution and the use of law enforcement resources has become a real consequence of the failure to pay.

> **FOR EXAMPLE:** Connecticut estimates that it has a deadbeat parent problem valued at $705.7 million. In the late 1990s, criminal sanctions began to be applied to the worst of these delinquent payors. In 1998, in one weekend, sheriffs in Connecticut tracked down and arrested more than fifty child support delinquents who allegedly owed more than $669,000.

Operations such as those conducted in Connecticut continue. In the fall of 2003, a federal crackdown of deadbeats in several states resulted in the arrest of more than one hundred parents who owed millions of dollars. These arrests were of people who had resources to pay, but did not. Parents rounded up included a university professor, a state official, and a divorce mediator. All these parents were charged with criminal complaints for willful failure to pay their court-ordered child support. Many had fled across state lines and switched jobs to avoid paying their debt. Most were at least one year overdue in their payments. Some had never made a single payment.

> **FOR EXAMPLE:** In an Ohio roundup in November of 2003, the state arrested 393 parents—one of those deadbeats owed $72,000. In May 2005, more than 150 deadbeat dads were arrested in a Mother's Day sweep in Cook County, Illinois. These dads cumulatively owed more than $1.6 million in overdue child support.

> A sheriff's office in Kentucky ran a sting called "Operation Nabbed," in which it sent six hundred delinquent parents a notice telling them that if they showed up to a certain location, they would get free cell

phone service from the Debban ("nabbed" spelled back-wards) company. The delinquent parents who showed up were arrested.

Another enforcement tool in Washington allows police to seize money from arrestees if the arrestee owes delinquent child support. By the end of 2003, $20,000 had been collected in this manner.

Within states, prosecutors can prosecute delinquent parents. On the federal level, the federal government estimates that billions of dollars in child support is owed to children whose parents have crossed state lines and failed to pay. It is a federal crime to fail to pay child support for a child living in another state. The Justice Department is now investigating and prosecuting cases in which parents cross state lines to avoid payment, and the amount owed is more than $5,000 or has remained unpaid for at least a year.

In order to prosecute, the United States Attorney's Office must prove that the paying parent was able to pay. Cases given priority include those in which there is a pattern of moving from state to state to avoid payment, or use of a false name or Social Security number.

**FOR EXAMPLE:** In June of 2005, after an executive businessman was arrested for failure to pay his out-of-state child support, he wrote a check for $57,000 to cover the full amount due. The father paid to avoid jail time on a felony charge.

# 7

# ENFORCING YOUR ORDER

Now that you understand some of the tools that exist to assist in collecting unpaid child support, you are ready to consider your options when the other parent stops paying on the order. Many parents do not pay because they think they will not get caught—not because they do not have the money. A recent study in California found that about 85% of cases being enforced by the state's child support agency had arrearages, with 80% of these parents having income, and some having money in bank accounts, credit unions, and other financial accounts.

Some cases are simply a matter of finding out the new address of a parent who moves across town. However, about one-third of parents who owe support move out of state. In these cases, it is more difficult and time-consuming to get enforcement, but certainly not impossible with the enforcement mechanisms available today.

## CONSIDER YOUR OPTIONS

You may choose to attempt to collect support owed by filing your own enforcement documents or you may choose to hire an attorney.

(See Chapter 12 on working with an attorney.) You can choose to hire one of the many private agencies that may, for a fee, attempt to collect past-due child support. Finally, you may turn to the local child support enforcement agency for assistance. Each of these methods has benefits and drawbacks.

Doing it yourself may be time-consuming and frustrating, but is fairly inexpensive. Paying attorneys or agencies is more costly, but they do the legwork. Public agencies may be the least expensive, but they often have large caseloads, and it may take more time and may not be as successful as focused private efforts to collect support.

The alternative you choose may involve some or all of these options. Each case must be evaluated in light of how difficult it will be to find the other parent and how hard the other parent tries to hide his or her assets.

> **FOR EXAMPLE:** One parent tried all of the options mentioned, with little success. A court order for support was entered when her son was 5 years old. Although she sought the services of a private agency, by the time her son had graduated college, she still had not received any support on the order. She got an attorney and obtained a $95,000 judgment for past-due support, but still received nothing from the father. It was only after the state of Illinois threatened to jail the defendant that he appeared in court to face his delinquency.

## Using a Private Agency

Private agencies are used by some parents to collect child support. If you consider hiring a private agency, you should be aware that they may charge around 30% of the support collected and may add additional fees. Some states are considering laws that limit what these agencies can charge.

Some companies may seek to collect fees even if the child support agency recovered the money by another means; for example, by intercepting a tax refund. You can check out a company by contacting your state's attorney general's office to see if there have been any complaints against the company.

A company may want you to sign a contract for its services. Be sure to read the fine print carefully before you sign to determine what the contract says. The company should not charge you large fees before they have provided any services. The company also should not charge you for work it did not do to recover past-due support.

It is important to be aware that a private collection agency may require that you close your case with the state child support agency as a condition of your contract. The federal Office of Child Support Enforcement warns that if you close your case with the state, the following collections services may not be available: tracking changes in the noncustodial parent's employment through the National Directory of New Hires; interception of state and federal tax returns and lottery winnings; passport denial; and, license revocation or suspension. (See the Information Memorandum developed by the federal Office of Child Support Enforcement if you are considering working with a private collection agency. It is available at **www.acf.hhs.gov/programs/cse**.)

## ARREARAGES

An *arrearage* is the amount of past-due child support. When some or all of the court-ordered child support is not paid, it begins to earn interest, and future payments must include this interest amount.

> **FOR EXAMPLE:** In Minnesota, if you do not pay your child support, you will have to pay your regular amount of support plus an additional 20% of your

child support order that will be applied to the past-due amount. You will also be charged interest on any past-due child support.

There is a major difference between past-due and current child support in the way courts treat enforcement.

> **FOR EXAMPLE:** The Utah Supreme Court, in *Utah v. Sucec*, 924 P.2d 882 (Utah 1996), decided that the current duty to support a child is owed to the child and not the custodial parent. The custodial parent cannot discharge, negotiate, or assign that ongoing obligation. However, child support arrears belong solely to the custodial parent as the one who provided the support to the child for the period that current support was not being paid.

Because the arrearage debt does not belong to the child, the custodial parent is free to discharge, negotiate, or assign that arrearage.

## ORDER FOR WITHHOLDING

Using an *order for withholding* is probably the best method used to ensure collection of child support. In fact, over 70% of cases in which child support is collected use this method. In one study in Colorado, where there was no order for withholding, only about 18% of parents paid support.

An order for withholding is easy to get when the child support order is first entered. The order tells an employer to automatically deduct the sum of the order (and an additional amount towards the arrearage, if any exist) every pay period, and send it either to the custodial parent or the state central registry for disbursement.

If the parties did not originally ask for an order for withholding to be entered, it is easy to go back to court and ask for one if payments stop. It is one of the most effective tools to get payments. Federal law caps the amount that can be withheld to a percentage of disposable income, depending on whether the paying parent has a second family and the paying parent's payment history. Arrearages are capped as follows:

| Past-due Support | Less than 12 weeks | More than 12 weeks |
| --- | --- | --- |
| No other family | 60% disposable income | 65% disposable income |
| A second family | 50% disposable income | 55% disposable income |

Many states follow federal limits, but some provide for a lesser amount.

Withholding can be used in enforcing a support order even if the paying parent lives in another state. The certified copy of the order is simply sent directly to the employer of the paying parent under new federal laws.

States use various forms for the order. A sample form can be found on the following pages.

# SAMPLE ORDER FOR WITHHOLDING

IN THE _____ COURT _____ , STATE

Petitioner,      )
v.            ) No. _____
Respondent.   )

## ORDER FOR WITHHOLDING

To:   Respondent's  Employer   _____
_____(name and address

Respondent's Social Security Number:_____

This **Order for Withholding** for Payment of Child Support is issued pursuant to the provision
of _____ state as a means of child support enforcement.

It is therefore ORDERED by this Court as follows:
1. The respondent is Ordered to pay the sum of $ _____
   per_____ as current , continuing child support an
   $ _____ per _____ toward the total chil
   support arrearage of $ _____.
2. The respondent's present employer or any future employer is hereby ordered to withhol
   from income due or to become due the respondent $ _____ p
   _____ for current continuing child support and $ _____ p
   _____ for child support arrearages which total $ _____
3. THE TOTAL AMOUNT OF ALL CHILD SUPPORT PAYMENTS TO BE WITH
   HELD IS $ _____ per _____, BUT SHALL NOT EXCEE
   _____ % OF THE RESPONDENT'S _____ INCOM
   SHOULD THE TOTAL AMOUNTS TO BE WITHHELD EXCEED THE PERCENT
   AGE OF THE RESPONDENT'S INCOME, THE PRIORITY OF WITHHOLDING I
   AS FOLLOWS:_____. When the Tot
   Arrearage(s) have been withheld and remitted to the above-named payee, DEDUCT ONL
   CURRENT CONTINUING SUPPORT until further instructed by this Court.
4. Respondent's employer shall remit the total amount deducted monthly to_____
   (payee) within ten (10) days of the date the respondent is paid the pay check from which th
   support is to be withheld at _____ (address). If the responde
   employee's pay periods are at intervals which are more frequent than once each month, th
   employer may withhold at each pay period an amount cumulatively sufficient to equal th
   total monthly support obligations and remit such amount withheld at each pay period t
   _____ (payee) within ten (10) days of the date the respondent is pai
   the pay check from which the amount is withheld.
5. This order shall be binding upon the respondent's employer/any successive employers fou
   teen (14) days after service pursuant to the Rules of Civil Procedure of this state and sha
   remain effective until further order of the Court.

6. A copy of this Order shall: Be served immediately upon the respondent's employer at (address)_____
   by:
   (Circle one)   personal service     certified mail
7. Costs of entering this order for income withholding are to be paid by:
   (circle one) Petitioner      Respondent      Waived
8. The respondent, the respondent's employer/any successive employers must notify _____ at (address) _____ of any changes in employment or termination of income/benefits.
9. The employer shall not use this Order as a basis for the discharge of the respondent/employee.
10. This order shall not under any circumstances be waived by mutual agreement of the parties.
11. An employer/successive employer who willfully fails or refuses to withhold or pay the amounts as ordered may be found to be in contempt of court. Additionally, such employer/successive employer may be found to be personally liable to the obligee for failure to answer or withhold and in such cases, conditional and final judgment for the amounts ordered to be withheld, may be entered by the court against the employer.
12. When the support payments are ordered paid directly to the Clerk of this Court, there shall be paid an additional $_____ administrative fee as provided by state law with each periodic payment.

The Clerk is hereby directed to mail a copy of this Order to the Clerk of the _____ Court of _____(state)_____which entered the original Order of support, and to further notify the clerk when this Withholding Order is served upon the employer and withholdings are to commence.

ENTERED:


_____     Date: _____
Judge

## ELECTRONIC FUNDS TRANSFER

Many states are moving to electronic funds transfer programs. Employers today provide about 70% of collections, and it is easier and cheaper to collect funds in this way. Through electronic funds transfer, funds are transferred online into designated accounts for distribution. As of 2005, twenty-two states provide the paying parent the opportunity to pay electronically.

## LENGTH OF TIME TO COLLECT

Some states do not impose a statute of limitations (time limit) within which to collect on past-due child support, but most do. Each state varies.

> **FOR EXAMPLE:** In Alaska, like many states, the time frame in which to go back to collect past-due child support is ten years after the child turns 18 years old. Idaho allows five years after the age of majority, so the action must be filed before the child turns 23 years old.

Waiting too long to collect may prevent the case altogether, so in considering your options, make sure you are aware of the statute of limitations.

## CHILD COLLECTING ARREARS

Some states do permit an adult to sue for support he or she did not receive as a child.

> **FOR EXAMPLE:** In Arkansas, the child has a right to sue for arrearages. (See Ark. Code Ann. Sec. 9-14-105.) In Mississippi, either the child or the custodial parent has the

right to bring an action against the defaulting parent for child support arrearages. (See *Brown v. Brown*, 822 So.2d 1119 (Miss. App. 2002).)

However, other states do not permit a child to collect an arrearage.

**FOR EXAMPLE:** In Oklahoma, the court in *Moore v. Moore*, 79 P.3d 1137 (Ok. App. 2003) said that the underlying reason that an adult child cannot sue for support is that payment of arrearage can be assumed to be a payment to reimburse the custodial parent for support of the children, rather than a payment for the benefit of the children themselves.

## FAILURE TO PAY AND VISITATION

The issues of child support and *visitation*, or parenting time, are very different. Failure to pay support is not a basis for failing to make a child available for court-ordered visits. The concealment of the child from the noncustodial parent may actually relieve the obligation to pay child support.

A court recently refused to permit a mother to collect court-ordered child support after she took and concealed the child from the father for a period of thirteen years. In this case, the mother obtained a child support order, but then moved out of state and left no forwarding address. Thirteen years later, she requested her state to begin collection on the order. The father's wages were assigned and an arrearage of more than $35,000 was assessed. The father paid the arrearage. The court, though, found that he was relieved of his duty to pay because of the concealment, which lasted until the child turned age 18. (*Stanislaus County Dept. of Child Support Services v. Jensen*, 112 Cal. App. 4th 453 (2003).)

# 8

# MODIFICATION

While an existing child support order is always subject to modification, it is important to recognize that modifications are not automatic. Either parent may seek a modification, upward or downward, of child support. To do so, however, requires the parent seeking the modification to return to a court (or administrative agency, if permitted) and obtain a new order.

To obtain some stability, most states require some period of time to pass (two or three years is common), or that the person seeking the modification show a *substantial change in circumstances* that warrants a review of the child support order.

> **FOR EXAMPLE:** In Washington, a child support order may be modified upon the request of a party if the order is at least twelve months old and if the order is a hardship on a parent or the child. All child support orders are adjustable every two years if the incomes of the parties change.

Typical reasons for requesting a review may include:
- a change in the gross income or employment status of either parent;
- when an order needs to be amended because medical support is not a part of the current support order;
- when extraordinary medical expenses for the child occur; and,
- when a change in the family's size occurs.

In Minnesota, you can seek to increase your child support order by filing a motion demonstrating a substantial change in circumstances. This usually requires a showing that the order should be increased under the guidelines by at least 20% and a minimum of $50. Unlike some states, Minnesota provides for an automatic increase in child support every two years based on an increase in the cost of living. The other parent will be notified and has an opportunity to object.

## SUBSTANTIAL CHANGE IN CIRCUMSTANCES

In most states, it will be considered a substantial or significant change in circumstances if the guideline amount at the time of the original order resulted in a child support payment order that is substantially different than what a current payment would be under the new guideline amount.

> **FOR EXAMPLE:** In Arizona and Florida, the person seeking the modification is required to show a variance of 15% or more from the existing amount. In Florida, the 15% must equal at least a $50 difference.
>
> In Vermont, the change required for a modification of child support must be a "real, substantial, and unanticipated change in circumstances," and must result in a change of at least 10% between the current

order and the amount calculated under the child support guidelines (not a 10% change in income).

Some states, such as Arizona, permit a simplified proceeding. To show this variation requires a parent to provide the court with a document proving the variance that will then be served upon the other parent. If no hearing is requested by the other parent, a court can simply review the request and enter the change in the order. If the matter is contested, there will be a hearing on the issue of the variance.

> **FOR EXAMPLE:** In Texas, only a court can modify child support. It cannot be done by agreement of the parties. Grounds for modification include a material and substantial change in the circumstances of a child or the parent, or the passage of at least three years since the last child support order, and the monthly payment differs by either 20% or $100 from the child support guidelines.

## PROCEDURES

To obtain modification in most states, you must obtain a certified copy of the current support order, complete the necessary petition or form application for a modification, pay a fee (unless waived or not required), and file the forms with the child support agency or a court. Some states require copies of your tax returns or pay stubs to be filed, but these are filed with a special form and kept sealed by the court. They should not be filed without the necessary confidential forms.

In South Dakota, you file a petition asking to modify child support. There is no fee for this petition. The petition includes information on the parent seeking the change (the petitioner) and the last known information on the other parent (the respondent). The petition includes information on the date and terms of the original order of child support. A copy of the order must accompany the petition. The reason for the modification request—that at least three years have passed or that there has been a substantial change in circumstances—must be listed. The petitioner can seek an increase or decrease in child support as circumstances dictate.

One reason to request a reduction is where there is shared parental responsibility or the noncustodial parent has obtained increased visitation. One reason to request an increase is because of increased child care costs for the custodial parent as a result of a job search, training, or education.

The petition must be accompanied by a signed financial statement listing the income and assets, allowable deductions, health insurance information, and applicable child care costs. Income must be verified with a copy of recent pay stubs.

In addition, in accordance with federal regulations, a child support order filing data form must be filed with the state central registry. This form allows the state to keep a record of information on both parties as well as the names, dates of birth, and Social Security numbers of any children. If there is a domestic violence protective order, the state registry will keep the protected party's information confidential.

Washington allows parents who agree to a modification to skip most of the paperwork and file an updated parent registry information form and a set of forms including an agreed petition for modification of child support, findings and conclusions on the petition for modification of child support, order on modification of child support, order of child support, child support worksheets, and a sealed financial source documents cover sheet with financial documents attached. These forms are then presented to a judge or commissioner for approval.

If the parents do not agree, a petition for modification of child support, supporting financial documents and worksheets, and the necessary filing fee must be filed in the local court. The documents (except for the confidential information sheet) are then served on the other parent. The respondent has twenty days to respond if in state or sixty days if out of state. Service by mail may be permitted under certain circumstances.

The petitioner cannot serve the documents him- or herself. Once the documents have been served, the respondent can answer the petition and provide his or her own financial documents and worksheets. If no response is filed within the appropriate time frame, a default judgment may be entered against the respondent. If the response has been filed on time, the case is then set for a review by a judge, who will make the decision on modification by examining all the documents provided. There is an opportunity to make written statements to the court, but in-person testimony is not usually permitted. The necessary forms are available on the Internet through the court's website.

**NOTE:** *Always keep copies of whatever you send to the court.*

## PAST-DUE SUPPORT

Modification of a past-due child support amount is not permitted by federal law. Modification can only be for future payments, so if a significant change in circumstances prevents payment of support, you must file your documents seeking a downward modification (or suspension) of support as soon as possible. If you lose your job, make less money than you used to, or become physically disabled and unable to earn an income, you must notify the court immediately or else the support will become due. Your excuse, however legitimate, will not reduce the past-due support. Prompt notice of your change in circumstances will allow a court to temporarily or permanently reduce the amount of future payments.

## REMARRIAGE

The second marriage of a parent will not impact a child support order, but new obligations to children will often result in that parent seeking modification of the order. Many states provide, in their schedule of guidelines, computations for factoring in a second child's obligations.

## CHANGE OF JOB

A parent's change in employment may be considered for a modification of future child support. However, if unemployment or underemployment results from an intentional choice or willfulness of the parent, the court may refuse to grant such a request.

## CHANGE OF CUSTODY

A change in the parenting of a child will often be grounds for modification of a child support order. Keep in mind, however, that this is not automatic. The child support order will not be modifiable until your petition to modify it is filed with the appropriate agency or clerk of the court.

## AGE OF MAJORITY OF ONE CHILD

Unless decreased automatically under state law, an order that includes a general support amount for multiple children does not automatically decrease when the oldest child reaches the age of majority. The paying parent cannot, on his or her own, reduce the payment by the percentage that one child reaching the age of majority would represent.

> **FOR EXAMPLE:** If the order covered three children, when the oldest reaches the age of 18, the paying parent cannot reduce his or her payment by one-third. He or she must return to court for modification to the order.

Today, many jurisdictions have a form to be used for changing a child support order. Check your own jurisdiction first for a form. A sample petition for modification of child support can be found on pages 118–119.

# SAMPLE PETITION FOR MODIFICATION OF CHILD SUPPORT

IN THE _____ COURT _____ , STATE

Petitioner,           )
v.                    ) No. _____
Respondent.           )

## PETITION FOR MODIFICATION OF CHILD SUPPORT

The ( ) Petitioner ( ) Respondent, _____, states as follows:

1. On _____, _____ was ordered to pay child supp
for _____ whose date of birth is _____.

2. The order of child support should be modified for the following reasons.

( )The previous order was entered more than ___ years ago and there has beer
change in the income of the parents.

( )_____ [Name of child] is in need of postse
ondary educational support because the child is in fact dependent and is relying upon the p
ents for the reasonable necessities of life.

( )_____ [Name of child] is a dependent ad
child and support should be extended beyond his or her eighteenth birthday.

( )The previous order was entered by default.

( )The previous order was entered more than a year ago and:

( )The order works a severe economic hardship.

( )The child has moved to a new age category for support purposes.

( )The child is still in high school and there is a need to extend support beyo
the child's eighteenth birthday to allow the child to complete high school.

( )Either or both parents should be required to maintain or provide health insurar
coverage.

( )There has been the following substantial change of circumstances since the order v
entered (explain):_____

WHEREFORE, [ ] PETITIONER OR [ ] RESPONDENT hereby requests this Court to:

3. Enter an order establishing child support in conjunction with the proposed child su
port worksheet and financial declaration which have been filed with this petition.

4. Other:

( )order child support payments which are based upon the State Child Supp
Guidelines. A copy of the child support worksheet is filed with this action.

( )require a periodic adjustment of support.

( )extend child support beyond _____
[Name of child] eighteenth birthday to allow the child to complete high school.

( )extend child support beyond _____
[Name of child] eighteenth birthday until (he) (she) is no longer dependent up
either or both parents and is capable of self-support.

( )allow for postsecondary educational support for _____
[Name of child].

( )order the payment of day care.
( )order the payment of educational expenses.
( )order the payment of long distance transportation expenses.
( )order the payment of uncovered health care expenses.
( )award the tax exemption for the children as follows:

_____

_____

_____

Dated: _____

Signature: _____

**ACKNOWLEDGMENT**

STATE OF _____ )ss

COUNTY OF _____ )

I, _____, being first duly sworn upon my oath, depose and state that I am the Petitioner in the above-entitled cause. I have read the attached PETITION TO MODIFY CHILD SUPPORT. I state that the contents thereof are true and correct, except to the matters stated on information and belief, and those matters I believe to be true.

_____

Signature of Party

SUBSCRIBED AND SWORN TO before me on this day: _____.

My Commission Expires: _____

_____

NOTARY PUBLIC

# 9

# TERMINATION

Like modification, certain events can trigger a termination of child support. Also like modification, termination may not be automatic.

## ADOPTION

The adoption of the child by the new spouse of the custodial parent may operate to terminate a child support order. This is because the adoption operates to legally establish a new father or mother for a child, and terminates all rights of the former parent.

## EMANCIPATION

The general rule is that courts do not usually award support for a child once he or she attains the age of majority (usually 18 or 21). As stated previously, however, the parties may agree to pay for the child's support for educational purposes, or for some other reason, until a specified event or date.

If there is more than one child covered by a support order, the emancipation of one child automatically is reduced proportionately by most states. However, in some states, the order is not reduced unless the parent responsible for payment seeks a reduction.

Even though a child turns 18 years of age, the law may not consider him or her emancipated.

> **FOR EXAMPLE:** In *Patetta v. Patetta*, 817 A.2d 327 (N.J.Super. 2003), the appellate court denied a father's request to terminate child support for one of his three children when the child turned 18. The mother objected since the child remained at home and attended a community college. The court found that there was no specific age at which a child would be considered emancipated in New Jersey. Reaching age 18 was considered, but the fact that the child remained in college full-time meant that the child was not able to live on his own. Even though the parties had an agreement to end child support at age 18, the court believed the right to support was the child's, so the mother could not bargain that support away.

## MARRIAGE OF THE CHILD

Marriage operates as an emancipation event. Even if the child is still considered a minor under the law, the child support order will terminate upon his or her marriage.

## SERVICE IN THE MILITARY

Enlisting in the military is usually seen as an emancipation event, even if the child is still a minor under the law. This operates to terminate a child support order in most states.

## DEATH OF PAYING PARENT

The death of a parent who has a duty to pay will generally not terminate the child support order. Even if the order does not terminate, the death of the party owing support will usually be grounds for seeking a modification of the order.

> **FOR EXAMPLE:** Out of the deceased parent's estate, the amount calculated to be due for support may be determined and converted into a lump-sum payment. If the deceased parent owes past-due child support, that can also be made a claim against that parent's estate.

A *Sample Petition for Termination of Child Support* appears on page 124.

## BANKRUPTCY

Ordinarily, when a person files for bankruptcy, efforts to collect on debts owed must stop. This is called an *automatic stay*. However, bankruptcy does not terminate past-due child support. (See 11 U.S.C. Sec. 523.) Also, changes to the bankruptcy laws in 2005 make it easier to establish and collect child support. For example, the filing of a bankruptcy petition has no effect on a parent's ability to file an action for child support (or custody or paternity) and the court can set the amount of child support immediately. Also, child support has a priority for payment. A discharge in bankruptcy will not affect the child support order, because bankruptcy cannot discharge child support. There are more complex rules regarding bankruptcy and child support, which are beyond the scope of this book. If a parent is considering filing for bankruptcy, contact an attorney familiar with these laws for assistance. (See Chapter 12 on working with an attorney.)

# SAMPLE PETITION FOR TERMINATION
# OF CHILD SUPPORT

IN THE _____ COURT _____ , STATE

Petitioner,         )
v.                   ) No. _____
Respondent.    )

## PETITION FOR TERMINATION OF CHILD SUPPORT

The Petitioner , _____, states as follows:

I am paying support in this case for the following child: _____ whose date of birth is _____. The child is no longer entitled to child support for the following reason:

    ( )The child died on _____; a certified death certificate is attached.

    ( )The child married on _____; a certified copy of the marriage license is attached.

    ( )The child entered active military duty on _____; verification is attached.

    ( )The child has attained the age of _____ or has been emancipated; verification is attached.

    ( )Other: (explain) _____.

WHEREFORE, PETITIONER hereby requests this Court to:
Enter an order terminating the child support.
Dated: _____ Signature: _____

## ACKNOWLEDGMENT

STATE OF  _____ )ss
COUNTY OF _____ )
I,_____, being first duly sworn upon my oath, depose and state that I am the Petitioner in the above-entitled cause. I have read the attached PETITION TO TERMINATE CHILD SUPPORT. I state that the contents thereof are true and correct, except to the matters stated on information and belief, and those matters I believe to be true.

_____

Signature of Party

SUBSCRIBED AND SWORN TO before me on this day: _____.
My Commission Expires: _____.

_____

NOTARY PUBLIC

# 10

# APPEAL

If child support is contested, either parent can file a request for an appellate court to review a trial court's child custody order.

Rarely does an appellate court reverse a child support decision. This is because, if the child support amount is within the guidelines, there is discretion for the trial court to make an award that is *just* and *equitable*. These terms are very broad, and a reviewing court would have to find that the trial court abused its discretion in entering the support order. This is a hard standard to meet, especially if the child support order is within or near the guideline amount, or if any deviation is supported with evidence demonstrating a financial need for more support.

Since courts rarely order a child support award under the guideline amount, appeals in these situations are also infrequent.

# 11

# FINDING THE LAW

The child support laws of every state differ, but all are found in each state's codes. To find the laws for your state, you will need to do some basic legal research.

## LAW LIBRARIES

A large public library may carry legal books, but a specialized law library will have the most up-to-date version of your state's laws, as well as other types of research materials not found in a regular public library. Law libraries are often found at or near courthouses. Your court clerk's office should be able to tell you the location of the nearest law library. Also, all law schools have law libraries.

Contact the closest appropriate library to determine hours and location. Ask whether there are any restrictions on the use of the library by the public. Some libraries may have restricted hours for nonlawyers or prohibit use by nonstudents. The reference librarians at the libraries are very good and can help you find the set of books you are looking for. (However, many county-funded law libraries cannot afford to staff a law librarian.) Bring a copy of the relevant page for your state found in Appendix B.

## STATE CODES OR STATUTES

Every state has passed a set of statutes or codes that contain the laws passed by the legislature that govern the determination of parentage and child support. Your first step will be to find the law in your state's statutes or codes.

The actual title of the set of books is very important; for example, *Arizona Revised Statutes Annotated* or *Delaware Code Annotated*. Refer to the listing in Appendix B for the exact title used in your state. Once you find the titles, look for the section numbers listed in Appendix B for your state to find the exact provisions of the law.

For example, if you look at the listing for Illinois in Appendix B, you will see the following notation after the heading, "The Law: Illinois Compiled Statutes (ILCS)." This gives you the title of the set of books (Illinois Compiled Statutes). You will also note the notation under the heading "Child Support: 750 ILCS 5/505." This tells you that the portion of the Illinois law relating to child support is found in Chapter 750 of the set of books called the *Illinois Compiled Statutes* and begins with Article 5, Section 505. The legal *citation* (abbreviation) for this would be "750 ILCS 5/505," where 750 refers to Chapter 750, "ILCS" is the abbreviation for Illinois Compiled Statutes, and "5/505" refers to Article 5, Section 505.

Once you locate the specific laws for your state, check to see if there is a more current version available. This may be in the form of an update inserted in the back of the volume, a separate update volume, or in some other format. If necessary, ask a reference librarian for assistance in order to be certain that you have the most recent version. The statutes may also be *annotated* with short summaries of court decisions that have interpreted the statutes.

## CASE REPORTERS

If you wish to find the court's entire decision, it will be included in a state or regional case reporter. A state case reporter, such as the *Illinois Reporter*, contains court opinions from the courts of a single state. A regional reporter, such as the *Northeastern Reporter*, contains cases from the courts of several states in a particular geographic area. To find a case, carefully copy down the case name and the numbers that follow it (called the citation), or make a copy of the page containing the case information. Next, locate the case reporters in the library. Many states have more than one reporter in which the same case can be found. Ask your reference librarian for assistance. The citation often looks as follows:

*In re Marriage of Sobol*, 342 Ill.App.3d 623, 796 N.E.2d 183 (2003)

| (name of case) | (state reporter) | (regional reporter) | (year pub.) |

Once you find the proper state or regional reporter, the citation is found using the following method:

| 342 | Ill.App. | 3d | 623 |
|---|---|---|---|
| (volume) | (state court) | (series) | (page number) |

You will find the Illinois appellate court opinion in the case of *In re the Marriage of Sobol* in volume 342 of the state reporter titled *Illinois Appellate Reporter, Third Series* on page 623.

After a point, instead of continuing to increase the volume numbers, publishers have started over with volume one of a subsequent *series* of the reporter. In the example, you would actually find three sets of books on the library shelves: one titled *Illinois Appellate Reporter*; another titled *Illinois Appellate Reporter, Second Series*; and a third titled *Illinois Appellate Reporter, Third Series*. Each set begins with "Volume 1." The third series contains the most recent cases.

## INTERNET RESEARCH

Increasingly, the Internet is becoming a resource to obtain legal information specific to the various states. Many states include their statutes (and selected cases) in their government Web pages. One easy way to find available Web information on the laws of your state is to begin by searching the *LawCrawler* search engine by Findlaw. Type in **www.findlaw.com**, then choose state cases and codes to search your state.

The Internet site for the Office of Child Support Enforcement can be found at **www.acf.dhhs.gov/programs/cse**. It provides links to states that have their own child support home pages. Some states also include child support forms in their family law or domestic relations area on their sites.

Researching on the Internet can be much faster than looking up your state's laws in the books, but online research produces only a screen snapshot at a time, so you may need to open several pages to see the whole picture of your state's laws. Also, be aware that information on a website may not be the most current version of the law.

When working online, be sure to review all of the relevant website information, then download or print the portion of the law you are interested in.

## LEGAL ENCYCLOPEDIAS

You should also be able to find sets of books called *legal encyclopedias* at a law library. These are similar to a regular encyclopedia—you look up the subject (child support) and it gives you a summary of the law on that topic, and it also provides citations to related cases. There are two national legal encyclopedias—*American Jurisprudence* (abbreviated *Am. Jur.*) and *Corpus Juris Secundum* (abbreviated *C.J.S.*). Many states have their own legal encyclopedias. Like the case reporters, these may have a second series.

## DIGESTS

Another type of book found in a law library is a digest. Like a legal encyclopedia, you look up the subject and instead of giving you a summary of the law, it gives you summaries of court cases discussing that topic. Look for a digest that is specific to your state; for example, *California Digest*. These may also have a second series.

## FORM AND PRACTICE MANUALS

All law libraries also have certain form and practice manuals that include the law, procedures, and forms used in your state. These can be very helpful in finding and preparing forms you may need. Never hesitate to ask a reference librarian for assistance in finding the practice section for family law in your legal library.

# 12

# THE ROLE OF
# LAWYERS

Cases involving getting, collecting, and modifying child support are considered civil cases (although in some cases, delinquencies are punished as criminal cases). For many years, if a party wanted a lawyer in this kind of case, that party would have to hire and pay for one him- or herself. Today, that is often still true.

However, in some cases, the effort to make parents responsible for child support has led to collection laws enforced by government attorneys who work for state or local child support enforcement agencies. The government attorney does not represent the parent seeking to establish a support order. Instead, the government attorney represents the interests of the state. There are also low- or no-cost legal service agencies that provide representation to eligible parents, usually based on low-income guidelines.

For most parents, cases involving the issues of child support are filed by the parties without the assistance of a government attorney. In these cases, it is still up to the parties to decide if they want to be represented by a lawyer. In choosing a lawyer, recognize that the law is a business as well as a profession. This usually means if you want a lawyer to help you obtain or collect child support, you will usually have to pay for one. However, if you are without funds to pay for an attorney, a court may order the parent with the most financial resources to pay for the attorney's fees of the other parent in some family law cases.

As you are evaluating your options with a lawyer, the lawyer is likely evaluating your case. Lawyers decide whether to take cases based on a number of factors, including the costs, time, effort, and potential for collection of fees.

## CONFIDENTIALITY

To encourage people to speak freely to their lawyers, the law provides confidentiality protection for clients. This is called the *attorney-client privilege*. The privilege prevents a lawyer from disclosing your information under most circumstances, so be honest in disclosing all the facts, even those facts about your marriage, your relationship with the other parent, or yourself that are embarrassing or humiliating. The lawyer will need this information to properly evaluate the case.

## FINDING A LAWYER

The search for a lawyer can take some time and no small amount of perseverance. Just as there are specialities in other professions, it is becoming rarer today to find a lawyer that has a general practice. Make sure that the lawyer you choose has some kind of experience in cases similar to yours. Many lawyers limit their practice to family law cases. Some states certify lawyers as specialists. For example, California qualifies certain lawyers as specialists in family law, which includes cases involving divorce, custody/visitation, and child support.

## Recommendations from Friends

Many times, a lawyer is chosen on the strength of recommendations by family or friends. These recommendations can be helpful because the good experience of your family member or friend may provide reliable information on the quality of service provided by the lawyer.

## Referral Services

If you do not personally know a lawyer and do not have a recommendation from a trusted friend or family member, you can look to other sources. In most cities there is a local *bar association* that is an organization to which many local attorneys belong. The bar association can help make lawyer referrals, either formally or informally. Sometimes, lawyers may list their practice in the Yellow Pages of the phone book under "Lawyer" or "Attorney."

## Prepaid Legal Plans

You may also be covered for family law matters under a prepaid legal plan. Under such a plan, you may qualify for a certain number of hours of consultation or services, or pay a reduced fee for certain services. A prepaid plan may be a benefit provided by your employer, or from an association, group, or union to which you belong. Be sure to check to see if you are covered by such a plan.

## Websites

Another area to search for finding a lawyer is on the Internet. Some lawyers now have Web pages, and list their services and contact information. One resource to check is **www.findlaw.com**. Even if you do not have access to the Internet at home, most public libraries have Internet computers for use by library patrons.

## Law Schools

Some law schools maintain clinical programs that take cases. Be sure to check with any area law schools to see if any programs exist and whether your case would be eligible for its service. If the clinic does accept your case, you might not be required to pay or you might have to pay on a sliding fee scale. This means that if you are charged at all, it will be an amount based on your income or ability to pay.

### Attorney Registration

Every state maintains a registration of lawyers who practice law within that state. To find the phone number and address of any lawyer within your state, contact the bar association or other attorney registration office within your state. To find your local bar association, simply look in the telephone Yellow Pages under "lawyer referrals."

## INITIAL CONTACT

The selection of a lawyer usually begins with a phone call. In this first contact with the lawyer, be sure to obtain some preliminary information and write it down as you collect it. Ask questions like the following.

- Does this lawyer charge for a consultation?
- How long will the first meeting be?
- How much does the lawyer usually charge for his or her services?

Compare the answers given by the lawyers you speak to, then decide which one to meet with for an initial consultation.

In some states, you can hire a lawyer to do a limited number of services. In this type of arrangement, the lawyer does not provide full-service representation, but may help you prepare forms or check them over, or may provide a certain level of advice.

## FIRST INTERVIEW

The first interview with a lawyer is very important. Remember that you have not agreed to anything other than the terms of the initial visit. Do not be intimidated by the thought of meeting with the lawyer. You are under no obligation to sign or agree to anything at this time, and you can take any written documents home to think about before you sign. Also, be sure to write down any information you obtain from the lawyer you speak to. It will help you remember who said what later.

Follow your instincts and trust your evaluation of the lawyer when you meet. Ask some of the following questions.

- Do you like this lawyer?
- Do you feel that he or she is listening to you and your situation?
- Are you treated with respect during your visit by the office staff?

Your gut will tell you much about whether you wish to proceed further with this lawyer.

In telling the lawyer about your case, be as clear and concise as possible. You will want to bring relevant documents that will help the lawyer to understand the facts of your case. Discuss what the lawyer thinks the projected costs will be and how you will be billed for those costs.

## FEE ARRANGEMENTS

In most types of family law cases, attorneys charge hourly fees in addition to the expenses of the case. Most attorneys are expensive, charging more than $100 per hour. Many require a substantial initial payment (sometimes called a *retainer*) from you to begin the case.

If a retainer is to be paid, make sure that you and your lawyer agree what minimum services are to be provided for that sum. For example, for a retainer of $500 or more, the lawyer should at least prepare and file your case, and have the petition served on the other parent.

What you want to avoid is a situation where you pay your lawyer a retainer, he or she writes a letter and makes a few phone calls to the other parent (or the parent's attorney), then tells you the retainer is used up and more money is required from you to continue your case.

In collection of past-due child support, some states permit attorneys to charge on a percentage of the judgment basis (usually one-third). If there is no judgment, then no fees will be due.

**NOTE:** *You will still be responsible to pay for the expenses of filing the documents, photocopying, telephone charges, postage, transcript, reporter, and service-type fees.*

Once your fee is arranged, make sure that you have it in writing so that there will be no confusion as to what is owed, and when and how it should be paid.

## WORKING WITH THE LAWYER

Once you decide to hire the lawyer and the lawyer agrees to take the case, be sure to let the lawyer know what kind of client you are. How involved do you want to be in the case? Do you want to be informed of each step in the case? Would you like copies of each document the lawyer files or receives in your case? Realize that you may be expected to pay for copies if there are costs involved. Alternatively, you may ask your lawyer to make the file available to you on a regular basis to view at his or her office, so you can keep up with developments in your case.

Your lawyer should be able to take you through the case step-by-step to explain the procedures and the anticipated timeline in your case. Ask the lawyer how often you can expect him or her to notify you about your case. If you know the general timeline of your case, it will help you understand how often to expect contact from the lawyer. For example, once your documents are filed with the court, it may be at least thirty days (or longer) before the other parent is required to file any response.

Set up a method of contact that is convenient for you and reasonable for your lawyer.

# EPILOGUE

Support is an entitlement of every child. Numerous laws have been passed in the past decade to help collect a staggering amount of unpaid child support. As states develop better procedures for finding parents, the goal of obtaining child support is evolving into a reality for millions of children.

Hopefully, you have learned something about your options for getting and enforcing a child support order. If you have been ordered to pay child support, consider the impact that the payment of support may have on your children, and do not seek to avoid your responsibility. Your children will thank you for this.

# GLOSSARY

## A

**acknowledgment of paternity/parentage.** A written form signed by the named father of a child born outside of marriage that he is the true father of the child.

**affidavit.** A statement signed under oath or by affirmation that is usually notarized.

**age of majority.** The age at which a child becomes an adult under state law. Each state may have slightly different ages for different purposes.

**arrearage.** Past-due, unpaid child support owed by the parent who has been ordered to pay child support.

## C

**child support enforcement agency.** An agency that exists in every state that finds absent parents; establishes, enforces, and modifies child support; and, collects and distributes child support money.

**child support guidelines.** A standard method states use for setting child support. Each state's guidelines may be different.

**complaint.** The written document filed in a court seeking to have parentage or child support established. This document can also be called a *petition* in some states.

**contempt.** A judicial determination that a person wilfully failed to follow the court's order.

**custodial parent.** The parent who has legal custody of a child.

**custody.** Legal custody is a determination by a court that establishes with whom a child will live. Physical custody describes with whom the child is living regardless of the legal custody status. Joint custody occurs when two persons share legal and/or physical custody of a child. Split custody occurs when two or more children are in the legal custody of different people. Some states use the concept of *parenting time* instead of custody.

# D

**default.** The failure of a defendant to file an answer or appear in court within the time limit after having been served with a summons and complaint. The failure to appear can then lead to a default judgment being entered by a court.

**defendant.** The person against whom a case is filed. This person may also be called a *respondent*.

**DNA.** The abbreviation for and standard term used for deoxyribonucleic acid, the genetic information of an individual.

# E

**electronic funds transfer (EFT).** The process by which money is transmitted electronically from one bank account to another.

**emancipation.** The age at which a parent is no longer responsible for the care of a child, usually because the child has reached the age of majority.

# F

**Federal Parent Locator Service (FPLS).** A service operated by the federal Office of Child Support Enforcement (OCSE) within the Department of Health and Human Services that obtains addresses, employer information, and data on child support cases in every state, compares them, and returns matches to the appropriate states. This helps state and local child support enforcement agencies locate absentee parents so that custody, visitation, and child support can be determined and enforced.

# G

**garnishment.** A legal action to withhold wages or other assets for payment of a debt.

**genetic (DNA) testing.** The analysis of blood or saliva to obtain genetic information that can identify the parents of a child.

# I

**income withholding.** The process by which an employer automatically deducts child support from income or wages. Income withholding is often incorporated into the child support agreement or order, and may be voluntary or mandatory.

# J

**judgment.** The decision or finding by a judge or administrative agency hearing officer that decides the issues (e.g., child support) in a case.

# L

**lien.** A claim upon property to prevent sale or transfer of that property until a debt is paid.

# M

**modification.** An increase or decrease in the amount of current child support due.

**motion.** A request by a party for an order from a court or hearing officer.

# N

**noncustodial parent.** The parent who does not have primary care, custody, or control of the child.

# O

**obligation.** The amount of money to be paid as child support by a parent.

**obligee.** The person or agency to whom child support is owed.

**obligor.** The person who is required to pay child support.

**Office of Child Support Enforcement (OCSE).** The federal agency responsible for the administration of the child support program. Created by Title IV-D of the Social Security Act in 1975, OCSE is responsible for the development of child support policies in the state child support enforcement programs.

# P

**parenting time.** *See custody.*

**paternity.** Legal determination of fatherhood. Paternity must be established before child or medical support can be ordered.

**payee.** The person or organization in whose name child support money is paid.

**payor.** The person who makes a payment, usually noncustodial parents or someone acting on their behalf.

**Personal Responsibility and Work Opportunity Reconciliation Act of 1996 (PRWORA).** The federal welfare reform law that provides a number of requirements for employers, public licensing agencies, and financial institutions, as well as state and federal child support agencies, to assist in the location of absent parents, as well as the establishment, enforcement, and collection of child support.

**petition.** A written document submitted to a court or administrative agency requesting a remedy, such as the establishment of child support.

**plaintiff.** A person who brings a case. This person may also be called a *petitioner.*

**pro se.** When a person chooses to act as his or her own attorney and represent him- or herself.

**public assistance.** State or federal programs, such as Temporary Assistance to Needy Families (TANF), that provide financial aid to eligible recipients.

# R

**respondent.** The party answering a petition. This person may also be called a *defendant.*

# S

**service by publication.** Serving notice of a case by publication in a newspaper, or by posting on a bulletin board of a courthouse or other public facility, when other types of service are impractical or have been unsuccessful. This procedure is not used in every state.

**service of process.** The delivery of a summons and complaint to a party for the purpose of obtaining jurisdiction over that party.

**State Parent Locator Services (SPLS).** Part of a state's child support enforcement agency, the SPLS locates absent parents in order to establish and enforce child support obligations, visitation, and custody orders, or to establish paternity.

**summons.** A notice to a defendant that an action against him or her has been filed in court, and that a judgment will be taken against him or her if the complaint is not answered within a certain time.

**support order.** An order setting the amount of child support. Support orders may also cover health care; payment of arrearages; or reimbursement of costs, fees, interest, and penalties.

# T

**Tax Refund Offset Program.** This federal program intercepts tax refunds and other federal monies, and reroutes the funds to pay past-due child support.

**Temporary Assistance to Needy Families (TANF).** Public assistance payments made to poor families, based on Title IV-A of the Social Security Act. The TANF program replaced Aid to Families with Dependent Children (AFDC) when the Personal Responsibility and Work Opportunity Reconciliation Act (PRWORA) was signed into law in 1996. Applicants for TANF benefits are automatically referred to their State IV-D agency in order to establish paternity and child support for their children from the noncustodial parent. This allows the state to recoup or defray some of its public assistance expenditures with funds from the noncustodial parent.

# W

**wage assignment.** A voluntary agreement by an employee to assign future wages to pay debts, such as child support.

**wage withholding.** A procedure by which scheduled deductions are automatically made from wages or income to pay a debt, such as child support. Wage withholding is often incorporated into the child support order, and may be voluntary or mandatory.

# APPENDIX A:

# Regional Offices of Child Support Enforcement

**REGION I—**

Connecticut
Maine
Massachusetts
New Hampshire
Rhode Island
Vermont

*OCSE Program Manager*
*Administration for Children*
*and Families*
John F. Kennedy
Federal Building
Room 2000
Boston, MA 02203
617-565-2440

**REGION II—**

New York
New Jersey
Puerto Rico
Virgin Islands

*OCSE Program Manager*
*Administration for Children*
*and Families*
Federal Building
Room 4114
Federal Plaza
New York, NY 10278
212-264-2890

## REGION III—
Delaware
Maryland
Pennsylvania
Virginia
West Virginia
District of Columbia

*OCSE Program Manager*
*Administration for Children*
*and Families*
150 South Independence Mall West
Suite 864
Philadelphia, PA 19106
215-861-4000

## REGION IV—
Alabama
Florida
Georgia
Kentucky
Mississippi
North Carolina
South Carolina
Tennessee

*OCSE Program Manager*
*Administration for Children*
*and Families*
Federal Center
61 Forsyth Street, SW
Suite 4M60
Atlanta, GA 30303
404-562-2960

## REGION V—
Illinois
Indiana
Michigan
Minnesota
Ohio
Wisconsin

*OCSE Program Manager*
*Administration for Children*
*and Families*
233 North Michigan Avenue
Suite 400
Chicago, IL 60601
312-353-4863

## REGION VI—
Arkansas
Louisiana
New Mexico
Oklahoma
Texas

*OCSE Program Manager*
*Administration for Children*
*and Families*
1301 Young Street
Room 914 (ACF-3)
Dallas, TX 75202
214-767-9648

## REGION VII—

Iowa
Kansas
Missouri
Nebraska

*OCSE Program Manager*
*Administration for Children*
*and Families*
601 East 12ᵗʰ Street
Federal Building
Suite 276
Kansas City, MO 64106
816-426-3584

## REGION VIII—

Colorado
Montana
North Dakota
South Dakota
Utah
Wyoming

*OCSE Program Manager*
*Administration for Children*
*and Families*
Federal Office Building
1961 Stout Street
9ᵗʰ Floor
Denver, CO 80294
303-844-1132

## REGION IX—

Arizona
California
Hawaii
Nevada
Guam

*OCSE Program Manager*
*Administration for Children*
*and Families*
50 United Nations Plaza
Room 450
San Francisco, CA 94102
415-437-8400

## REGION X—

Alaska
Idaho
Oregon
Washington

*OCSE Program Manager*
*Administration for Children*
*and Families*
2201 Sixth Avenue
Mail Stop RX-70
Seattle, WA 98121
206-615-2547

# APPENDIX B:

# State-by-State Parentage and Child Support Laws

The following section contains a state-by-state summary of the applicable laws relating to parenthood and child support, as well as the state agency to contact for information and assistance. While every effort has been made to provide up-to-date information, states often review and amend their laws concerning child support, so the information in this appendix can change at any time. Refer back to the section on legal research for more information on researching the law for your state.

For further information on states that have their own child support Internet home pages, you may also visit the Office of Child Support Enforcement on the Web at **www.acf.hhs.gov/programs/cse**.

## EXPLANATION
Following is an explanation of what information may be found under each of the headings in this appendix.

**Law:**
This section identifies the name of the set of books containing the laws passed in a particular state. The name is followed by the general citation of how the laws are referenced as will be specifically done in the following sections. The abbreviation "Sec." means "Section."

For some states, information is also given to try to help you find the specific volume or volumes you will need. For example, a direction to "ignore volume numbers" means that the books will give both a volume number and a section or chapter number on the cover. Use the section or chapter number and not the volume number. If the section number is followed by "et seq.," it means that the reference begins there and continues in several following sections in sequence.

**Paternity:**
This tells you where to look for the general presumptions pertaining to determining who the parents of a child are and gives a summary of what factors are considered in establishing parentage, how parents can agree to acknowledge paternity, and how that acknowledgment can be withdrawn.

**Child Support:**
This section tells you where to look for the general laws pertaining to child support for your state and gives a summary of how child support is calculated.

**Agency:**
This section gives the name and location of the central office of the child support agency in your state. There is most likely a local office, which you can locate by looking for the agency listed in your telephone directory in the government listings pages.

**Website:**
This gives you the current homepage of the state's child support enforcement agency. Many states' homepages also provide listings for local offices, helpful information concerning state-specific procedures, and some provide forms.

# ALABAMA

**Law:**
Code of Alabama. Ala. Code Sec. (Ignore volume numbers.)

**Paternity:**
Ala. Code Sec. 26-17-5. A man is presumed to be the father of a child: if the parties are married at time of birth or within 300 days thereof; if the man has attempted an invalid marriage to the mother before the birth of the child; if the man receives the child into his home or openly holds the child out as his during the child's minority; or, if he and the child's mother have acknowledged paternity in an affidavit of paternity.

Ala. Code Sec. 26-17-22. Provides for an acknowledgment of paternity, called an *affidavit of paternity*, to be signed by both parties before a notary public. The acknowledgment may be signed anytime prior to the child's 19th birthday. This section also provides for withdrawing the acknowledgment within the earlier of sixty days or the time a proceeding is filed related to the child. After that time, the challenger must prove in court that the acknowledgment was obtained by fraud, duress, or material mistake of fact. Child support is not stayed pending the challenge, absent good cause shown.

Ala. Code Sec. 26-17A. Allows reopening a paternity case upon DNA evidence. No money damages are allowed if paternity is vacated.

**Child Support:**
Alabama Rules of Judicial Administration 32. Guidelines for child support are used in any action to establish or modify child support, whether temporary or permanent. There shall be a rebuttable presumption that the guideline's amount is the correct amount of child support to be awarded. The guideline's amount can be modified up or down if the parties have a fair, written agreement establishing a different amount and stating the reasons therefor or there is a determination by the court, based upon evidence presented in court, stating that application of the guidelines would be manifestly unjust or inequitable. Reasons for deviating from the guidelines include shared physical custody or substantial visitation rights providing for periods of physical custody or care of children by the paying parent; extraordinary costs of transportation for purposes of visitation paid substantially by one parent; expenses of college education incurred prior to a child's reaching the age of majority; assets of, or unearned income received by or on behalf of, a child or children; and such, other facts or circumstances that the court finds contribute to the best interest of the child or children for whom support is being determined.

The basic child support obligation is determined by using the schedule of obligations. All orders establishing or modifying child support must provide for the children's health care needs, ordinarily through health insurance.

Child support is determined by adding the basic child support obligation, work-related child care costs, and health insurance costs. Child support is divided between the parents in proportion to their adjusted gross incomes. The obligation of each parent is computed by multiplying the total child support obligation by each parent's percentage share of their combined adjusted gross income. The custodial parent is presumed to spend his or her share directly on the child.

The guidelines are used to consider periodic modifications and modifications can only be as to child support due after the filing of the petition for modification. It is presumed that child support should be modified when the difference between the existing child support award and the amount determined by application of these guidelines varies more than 10%.

**Agency:**
Department of Human Resources
Division of Child Support
50 Ripley Street
Montgomery, AL 36130
334-242-9300
800-284-4347 (in-state only)

**Website:**
www.dhr.state.al.us

## ALASKA

**Law:**
Alaska Statutes. A.S. Sec. (Ignore volume numbers—look for "title" numbers.)

Supplement is in the front of each volume.

**Paternity:**
A.S. Sec. 25.20.050. A man is presumed to be father of a child if: the parties are married at time of birth or the man subsequently marries the mother of the child; the man acknowledges paternity; he and the child's mother have executed an acknowledgment under A.S. 18.50.165; or, the man is determined by a judge or appropriate agency to be a parent of the child on evidence that the man's words or actions indicate that he treated the child as his own.

A.S. Sec. 25.20.050(l). Provides that acknowledgment may only be withdrawn within sixty days. After this time period has passed, the acknowledgment may only be contested in court on the basis of fraud, duress, or material mistake. Unless good cause is shown, any child support order is not stayed while case is pending.

**Child Support:**
Alaska made numerous changes to its Civil Rule 90.3 in 2005. It also revised many of its court forms. For the lowest income payors, Alaska removed the minimum $50 amount and replaced it with a sliding fee scale. It also changed highest income caps. The seasonal income formula has been modified to reflect seasonal fluctuations in income.

Alaska uses a *net percentage of income* standard. Health insurance will be required for the children if insurance is available to either parent at a reasonable cost. In sole custody cases, the percentage by which the noncustodial parent's adjusted income must be multiplied in order to calculate the child support award is: 20% (1 child); 27% (2 children); 33% (3 children); and, an extra 3% for each additional child. In any period where the paying parent has over twenty-seven consecutive days of visitation, the order may be reduced by up to 75%. A court may impute income to a parent who is voluntarily and unreasonably unemployed or underemployed. A court may issue a written order departing from the guidelines amount for good cause upon clear and convincing evidence of manifest injustice if the guidelines were to be applied. Grandparents may be ordered to pay support under certain circumstances.

## Modification:

A final child support award may be modified upon showing of a material change of circumstances, which will be presumed if child support is more than a 15% variation of the outstanding support order. Ordinarily, child support arrearages may not be modified retroactively (except as allowed by A.S. 25.27.166(d)), however, modification can become effective back to the date of filing the request for modification.

## Agency:

Child Support Enforcement Division
550 West 7th Avenue
Suite 310
Anchorage, AK 99501
907-269-6900
800-478-3300 (in-state only)

## Website:

www.csed.state.ak.us

## ARIZONA

**Law:**
Arizona Revised Statutes. Ariz. Rev. Stat. Sec. (Ignore volume numbers; look for "section" numbers.)

**Paternity:**
Ariz. Rev. Stat. Sec. 25-814. A man is presumed to be the father if: he and the mother were married at any time ten months prior to the birth of the child or the child is born ten months after the marriage ends; if DNA tests show a 95% probability of paternity; if the parents are not married, but they both sign the birth certificate; or, if the parents sign an acknowledgment.

Ariz. Rev. Stat. Sec. 25-812. An acknowledgment must be notarized or witnessed, and signed by both parents. An acknowledgment filed with the appropriate agency has the same effect as a judgment of paternity.

Ariz. Rev. Stat. Sec. 25-812 E. Allows a person to withdraw the acknowledgment within the earlier of sixty days of the last signature on the document or a proceeding related to the child. After that period, the acknowledgment may only be contested in court on the basis of fraud, duress, or material mistake. A child support order is not suspended while the challenge is pending.

**Child Support:**
Supreme Court Administrative Order 96-29. Arizona adopted new guidelines in 2005. The guidelines follow the principal that the total support for a child should be in an amount that approximates what would have been spent on the child if the parents lived together. Arizona is a *combined adjusted gross income state*. Gross income includes income from any source, less public assistance benefits, certain self-employment expenses, and payments under prior orders for

child support and spousal maintenance. The adjusted gross income for each parent is added together to produce the combined adjusted gross income. The state schedule will show the amount of support due for this income level. Expenses for health insurance will be added and child care, education, older child, and other extraordinary expenses may be added to this support amount. Next, each parent's percentage share is determined by dividing the parent's adjusted gross income by the combined adjusted income. The result is that parent's share of the combined adjusted gross income. A visitation credit will be awarded to the parent without custody if that parent has a total annual amount of parenting time of three days or more. For example, a parent who has a child for sixty days will get an 8.5% credit adjustment subtracted from the child support due.

The parent without custody will be ordered to pay a certain amount while the parent with custody will be presumed to spend his or her proportionate share directly on the child. However, a court may order a custodial parent to pay child support in appropriate cases. There is a "self-support reserve" amount calculated to ensure that a paying parent will be financially able to pay the ordered amount. Upon written findings, a court may deviate from the guidelines where application of the guidelines is inappropriate or unjust for the particular case. By voluntary agreement, the parties may also deviate, if they recognize what the guidelines amount would have been and a court approves of the deviation.

Modification is permitted upon a showing of a substantial and continuing change of circumstances, such as a 15% difference between the amount ordered and the guidelines. The Rule sets out the procedure and forms required. Approved forms are available from the Clerk of the Superior Court.

**Agency:**
Division of Child Support Enforcement
P.O. Box 40458
Phoenix, AZ 85067
602-252-4045
800-882-4151 (in-state only)

**Website:**
www.de.state.az.us/dcse

# ARKANSAS

## Law:
Arkansas Code Annotated. Ark. Code. Ann. Sec. (Look for "title" or "chapter" numbers.)

## Paternity:
Ark. Code Ann. Sec. 9-10-109. The husband is presumed to be the father of a child. The court can determine paternity and enter a child support order upon a finding of paternity.

Ark. Code Ann. Sec. 9-10-120. An acknowledgment of paternity, called an *affidavit of paternity*, must be signed by both parties during the child's minority. An acknowledgment operates as a conclusive finding of paternity and creates a parent and child relationship between father and child.

Ark. Code Ann. Sec. 9-10-120. An acknowledgment of paternity can be withdrawn within the earlier of sixty days or at the commencement of a proceeding related to the child. After that period, the acknowledgment may only be contested in court on the basis of fraud, duress, or material mistake. Any child support order is not suspended while the challenge is pending, except upon good cause shown.

## Child Support:
Arkansas Administrative Order of the Supreme Court No. 10. The guidelines presume that the amount of child support calculated under the most recent revision of the Family Support Chart is the amount of child support to be awarded in any judicial proceeding for divorce, separation, paternity, or child support. The court may grant less or more support if the evidence shows that the needs of the children require a different level of support, but any deviation must be justified.

The guidelines provide a chart of support due based on number of children and income level. The court order must provide for the child's health care needs, which normally would include health insurance if available to either parent at a reasonable cost. Income means any form of payment, including wages, salaries, commissions, bonuses, worker's compensation, disability, pension and interest, *less* deductions for taxes, social security (FICA), Medicare, railroad retirement, medical insurance paid for dependent children, and presently paid support for other dependents by Court order. Visitation credit for extended visitation periods is permitted.

The court may not modify any child support judgment that has accrued unpaid support prior to the filing of the motion for modification. Further, modification of child support is applied only as of the date of filing and service of the request for modification on the other party.

**Agency:**
Office of Child Support Enforcement
P.O. Box 8133
Little Rock, AR 72203
501-682-8398
800-247-4549

**Website:**
www.state.ar.us/dfa/childsupport

# CALIFORNIA

**Law:**
*West's* Annotated California Codes, Family Code. Fam. Code Sec. (There is also a set called Deering's California Codes Annotated that will contain the same section numbers.)

**Paternity:**
Fam. Code Sec. 7611. A man is presumed to be father of a child if: the parties are married at time of birth or within 300 days thereof; the man has attempted an invalid marriage to the mother before the birth of the child; the man receives the child into his home or openly holds the child out as his during the child's minority; or, the man acknowledges paternity.

Fam. Code Sec. 7570-77. Provides for acknowledgment of paternity that must be signed by both parents.

Fam. Code Sec. 7575-7577. Either parent may file for rescission of acknowledgment by filing a rescission form with the Department of Child Support Services within sixty days of the date of the last signature, unless a court order for custody, visitation, or child support has been entered in an action in which the signatory seeking to rescind was a party. Any order for custody, visitation, or child support shall remain in effect until the court determines that the voluntary declaration of paternity should be set aside, subject to the court's power to modify the orders.

Fam. Code Sec. 7630. Allows reopening a paternity case if filed within two years of child's birth.

**Child Support:**
Fam. Code Secs. 4050–4076. The guidelines are presumptively the correct amount of child support. A court must justify any support amount that differs from the statewide uniform guideline formula amount. Reasons for a variation include: the parties have stipulated to a different amount of child support; the parent being ordered to pay child support has an extraordinarily high income and the amount determined under the formula would exceed the needs of the children; a party is not contributing to the needs of the children at a level commensurate with that party's custodial time; or, application of the formula would be unjust or inappropriate due to special circumstances in the particular case, such as, for example, cases in which the parents have different time-sharing arrangements for different children or children have special medical needs.

The amount of child support to be paid by parents is based on the amount of time each parent spends with the child and their net income. Net income is calculated by taking a person's total income and subtracting certain expenses, such as federal and state income taxes, health insurance premiums, state disability insurance, and Social Security taxes. A court may permit other expense deductions. The percentage of income payable is: 25% (one child), 40% (two children), and 50% for three children, which will then be adjusted according to the amount of time each parent spends with the child(ren). A court may also add in certain expense adjustments to child support, such as child care, medical bills not paid by insurance, travel expenses for visitation with the other parent, or a child's special education needs.

Modifications are permitted upon a significant change in circumstance. An order modifying or terminating a support order may be made retroactive to the date of the filing of the notice of motion or order to show cause to modify or terminate.

**Agency:**
Department of Child Support Services
P.O. Box 419064
Rancho Cordova, CA 95741
866-249-0773
800-615-8858

**Website:**
www.childsup.cahwnet.gov

## COLORADO

**Law:**

*West's* Colorado Revised Statutes Annotated. (Col. Rev. Stat. Ann. Sec.)

**Paternity:**

Col. Rev. State. Ann. Sec. 19-4-105. A man is presumed to be the natural father of a child if (1) he and the child's natural mother are or have been married to each other or (2) have attempted to marry but the marriage is invalid and the child is born during the marriage or within 300 days of the end of the marriage. Paternity can also be acknowledged by both parents in writing on a form filed with the court or registrar of vital statistics. If only the father signs the form, but the mother is notified and does not dispute the acknowledgment within a reasonable time after notice, the man is presumed to be the father. A man is also presumed to be the natural father of a child if: with his consent, he is named as the child's father on the child's birth certificate; or, he is obligated to support the child under a written voluntary promise or by court order or by an administrative order issued pursuant to section 26-13.5-110, Col. Rev. Stat. This presumption of paternity also exists if he takes the minor child into his home and openly holds out the child as his natural child.

Col. Rev. State. Ann. Secs. 19-4-105-107 and 25-2-112. The father has the earlier of sixty days or the commencement of a proceeding relating to the support of the child to withdraw his acknowledgment of paternity. After that time, paternity may be challenged in court only on the basis of fraud, duress, or mistake of material fact. Any legal responsibilities resulting from signing an acknowledgment of paternity, including child support obligations, shall continue during any challenge to the finding of paternity, except for good cause shown.

**Child Support:**
Col. Rev. Stat. Sec. 14-10-115. Child support is determined using the schedule of basic child support obligations in the guidelines. Child support will be divided between the parents in proportion to their adjusted gross incomes. "Adjusted gross income" means gross income less existing child support orders, alimony, or maintenance actually paid by a parent. Except in cases of shared physical custody or split custody, child support is determined by adding each parent's obligations for basic child support amount, work-related child care costs, extraordinary medical expenses, and extraordinary adjustments to the guideline schedule. The custodial parent is presumed to spend his or her child support directly on the children. The noncustodial parent will owe his or her total child support to the custodial parent minus any payments ordered to be made directly for the child such as extraordinary medical expenses, or extraordinary adjustments to the schedule. In shared custody cases, each parent's share of the adjusted basic child support obligation is multiplied by the percentage of time the children spend with the other parent to determine the basic child support obligation owed to the other parent. The parent owing the greater amount of child support shall owe the difference between the two amounts as a child support to the other parent. This figure can also be adjusted by certain expenses or direct payment sums.

Modification is permitted upon a showing of a substantial and continuing change of circumstances, such as at least a 10% difference between the amount ordered and the guidelines. Modification may be effective as of the date of the filing of the motion, unless the court finds that it would cause undue hardship or substantial injustice.

**Agency:**
Division of Child Support Enforcement
1575 Sherman Street
5th Floor
Denver, CO 80203-1714
303-866-4300

**Website:**
www.childsupport.state.co.us

# CONNECTICUT

## Law:

Connecticut General Statutes. Conn. Gen. Stat. Sec. (Ignore "chapter" numbers; look for "title" numbers.)

## Paternity:

Conn. Gen. Stat. Sec. 46b-160. A husband is presumed to be the father of a child born during the marriage.

Conn. Gen. Stat. Sec. 46b-172. A written acknowledgment of paternity executed and sworn to by the putative father of the child when accompanied by (A) an attested waiver of the right to a blood test, the right to a trial, and the right to an attorney, and (B) a written affirmation of paternity executed and sworn to by the mother of the child shall have the same force and effect as a judgment of court regardless of whether the parents are minors.

Conn. Gen. Stat. Sec. 46b-172(a)(2). A withdrawal of an acknowledgment is permitted within the earlier of sixty days or the date of an agreement to support such child or an order of support for such child. After that time, paternity may be challenged in court only on the basis of fraud, duress, or mistake of material fact. While any such challenge is pending, any responsibilities arising from such acknowledgment shall continue except for good cause shown.

## Child Support:

Conn. Gen. Stat. Sec. 46b-215a-2a. Connecticut has updated its child support guidelines in 2005. Child support guidelines now exclude low income parents (those earning less than $50 a week). The basic support obligation is determined by applying the combined net income of both parents and applying it to the guideline schedule. The parent who pays health insurance premiums is entitled to a deduction from gross income. Calculate each parent's share of the combined net income and multiply the result for each parent by the total obligation due. The custodial parent's amount due is presumed to be spent directly on the children. The noncustodial parent's amount due is the basic child support obligation. Shared custody arrangements may produce a different amount.

Modification is permitted upon substantial deviation (usually at least 15%) from the guideline amount.

**Agency:**
Department of Social Services
Bureau of Child Support Enforcement
25 Sigourney Street
Hartford, CT 06106
860-424-4989
888-233-7223
800-842-1508

**Website:**
www.dss.state.ct.us/svcs/csupp.htm

# DELAWARE

**Law:**
Delaware Code Annotated. Del. Code. Ann. tit. Sec. (Ignore volume numbers; look for "title" numbers.)

**Paternity:**
Del. Code Ann. tit.13 Sec. 804. A man is presumed to be the father of a child if: he and the mother of the child are married to each other (even if the marriage is invalid) and the child is born during the marriage or within 300 days after the marriage is terminated by death, annulment, declaration of invalidity, or divorce; after the birth of the child, he and the mother of the child married each other (even if the marriage is declared invalid) and he consented to have his name on the birth certificate or he has been ordered to pay child support; he voluntarily acknowledged his paternity of the child; or, while the child was under the age of majority, he took the child into his home and openly held out the child as his own.

Del. Code Ann. tit. 13 Sec. 8- 301. The mother of a child and a man claiming to be the genetic father of the child may sign an acknowledgment of paternity. The acknowledgment must be signed under oath. A minor may sign an acknowledgment of paternity.

Del. Code Ann. tit. 13 Sec. 8-304(c). The acknowledgment is binding and conclusive on the issue of paternity unless withdrawn by a parent by filing a claim in court within sixty days or be written rescission filed with the Office of Vital Statistics accompanied by the rescinding parent's affidavit showing notice to the other parent. An acknowledgment can be set aside by a court for fraud, duress, or material mistake of fact. If a parent is under the age of 18 when the acknowledgment is signed, the parent has sixty days from the date of his or her 18th birthday to rescind the acknowledgment.

**Child Support:**

Delaware Family Court Civil Rules. Delaware is a *combined net income* state that permits a deduction for self-support of a parent. From gross income is deducted withholding for taxes, FICA, medical insurances, retirement, union dues, and other permitted expenses. From the net income amount is also deducted a parent's self-support allowance, because each parent is entitled to keep a minimum amount of income for their own needs. The remaining sum is the net income available for child support. The primary support obligation is then determined by application to the guidelines for the correct number of children to be supported.

In determining the amount of support due to one to whom the duty of support has been found to be owing, the Court, among other things, shall consider: the health; relative economic condition; financial circumstance; income—the wages and earning capacity—of the parties, including the children; the manner of living to which the parties have been accustomed when they were living under the same roof; and, the general equities inherent in the situation.

A petition for modification of child support may be made if it has been thirty months or more since the last order. The order will be modified based on the Delaware Child Support Formula. No petition for modification may be filed before that time unless there has been a substantial change in circumstances that requires a change, upward or downward, of 10% or greater. An order of child support may not be retroactively modified except back to the date that notice of the petition for modification has been given to the paying parent or his agent.

**Agency:**
Division of Child Support Enforcement
Delaware Health and Social Services
84A Christina Road
P.O. Box 904
New Castle, DE 19720
302-577-7171
800-273-9500

**Website:**
www.state.de.us/dhss/dcse

## DISTRICT OF COLUMBIA

**Law:**
District of Columbia Code Annotated D.C. Code Ann. tit. Sec.

**Paternity:**
D.C. Code tit.16 Sec. 909. A man is presumed to be the father of a child if: the parties are married at time of birth or within 300 days thereof; the man has attempted an invalid marriage to the mother after the birth of the child and he has acknowledged the child to be his; or, the man acknowledges paternity.

D.C. Code Ann. tit.16 Sec. 909.01. Provides for acknowledgment of paternity by a signed document of both parties.

D.C. Code Ann. tit.16 Sec. 909.01(a)(1). Provides that an acknowledgment can be withdrawn within the earlier of sixty days or the time a proceeding is commenced relating to the child. An acknowledgment which has not been rescinded shall legally establish the parent-child relationship between the father and the child for all rights, privileges, duties, and obligations under the laws of the District of Columbia. The acknowledgment shall be admissible as evidence of paternity.

**Child Support:**
D.C. Code Ann. Sec. 16-916.1. Parties may agree on a support amount as long as they are aware of the guideline amounts, which are: 20% (one child), 26% (two children), 30% (three children), and 32% (four or more children). These guideline amounts are increased or decreased depending on the parent's gross income and the age of the child. Currently, the guidelines have five income levels with a different percentage applied at each level. The court may order, at any time, that maintenance or support payments be made

to the clerk of the court for remittance to the person entitled to receive the payments.

A modification of a support order may be made upon showing of a material and substantial change in the needs of the child or the ability of the paying parent to pay. Also, every three years the order is modifiable if the guidelines indicate that application of the guideline to the current circumstances of the parties will result in an amount of child support that varies from the amount of the existing child support order by 15% or more.

**Agency:**
Child Support Services Division
Office of the Attorney General
Judiciary Square
441 Fourth Street, NW
5th Floor
Washington, DC 20001
202-442-9900

**Website:**
www.csed.dc.gov/esed

## FLORIDA

**Law:**
Florida Statutes Annotated. Fla. Stat. Ann. Sec. (Ignore volume numbers—look for "chapter" numbers.)

**Paternity:**
Fla. Stat. Ann. Sec. 742.091. If a child is born outside of marriage to parents that later marry, the child will be presumed to be the child of the husband. In the case of unmarried parents, paternity may be established by acknowledgment or court order.

Fla. Stat. Ann. Sec. 742.10. A notarized voluntary acknowledgment of paternity shall create a rebuttable presumption of paternity and is subject to the right of any signatory to rescind the acknowledgment within sixty days of the date the acknowledgment was signed, or the date of an administrative or judicial proceeding relating to the child, including a proceeding to establish a support order in which the signatory is a party, whichever is earlier. After that time, a signed voluntary acknowledgment of paternity shall constitute an establishment of paternity and may be challenged in court only on the basis of fraud, duress, or material mistake of fact. The legal responsibilities, including child support obligations, of any signatory arising from the acknowledgment may not be suspended during the challenge, except upon a finding of good cause by the court.

**Child Support:**
Florida Statutes Annotated Sec. 61-13(a). The court initially entering a support order has jurisdiction to modify payments, when the modification is found necessary by the court in the best interests of the child, when the child reaches majority, or when there is a substantial change in the circumstances of the parties. An initial child support award may be retroactive for twenty-four months prior to the filing of the case. Support orders must contain provisions for health insurance

for the minor child when the insurance is reasonably available. The court shall apportion the cost of coverage, and any noncovered medical, dental, and prescription medication expenses of the child, to both parties by adding the cost to the basic obligation determined pursuant to Sec. 61.30(6). The court may order that payment of uncovered medical, dental, and prescription medication expenses of the minor child be made directly to the payee on a percentage basis.

If both parties request and the court finds that it is in the best interest of the child, support payments need not be directed through the county depository. The court shall provide a copy of the order to the depository. If there is a default in payments, any party may subsequently file an affidavit with the depository alleging a default in payment of child support and stating that the party wishes to require that payments be made through the depository. The party shall provide copies of the affidavit to the court and to the other party. Fifteen days after receipt of the affidavit, the depository shall notify both parties that future payments shall be paid through the depository.

Modification is permitted every three years or if there is a substantial change in circumstances, which is shown by a 15% or $50 amount in the application of the guidelines to the current award.

**Agency:**
Child Support Enforcement Program
Department of Revenue
P.O. Box 8030
Tallahassee, FL 32314
800-622-5437

**Website:**
www.state.fl.us/cf_web

## GEORGIA

**Law:**
Official Code of Georgia Annotated. Ga. Code Ann. Sec. (Ignore volume numbers—look for "title" and "chapter" numbers.)

**Paternity:**
Ga. Code Ann. Sec. 19-7-20. The father is presumed for all children born into a marriage and within the "usual gestational period" thereafter. If the child is born to the parties prior to marriage, and the father treats the child as his own, he is presumed to be the father and the child will have his surname. Paternity may also be established by court proceeding or by acknowledgment.

Ga. Code Ann. Sec. 19-7-46.1. An acknowledgment must be signed by both parties and once recorded in the putative father registry, is a legal determination of paternity. An acknowledgment can be withdrawn by either party prior to the date of the child support order, any other order adjudicating paternity, or sixty days from the signing of the agreement, whichever is earlier. After the sixty day rescission period, the signed voluntary acknowledgment of paternity may be challenged in court only on the basis of fraud, duress, or material mistake of fact. Child support obligations may not be suspended during the challenge, except for good cause shown.

Ga. Code Ann. Sec. 19-7-54. Allows a challenge to determination of paternity based on newly discovered evidence and DNA testing.

**Child Support:**
Ga. Code Ann. Sec.19-6-15. Child support is based on a percentage of gross income (100% of wages, interest, dividends, rental income, self-employment, and all other income, except need-based public assistance). The amount is determined by multiplying the gross income by a percentage based on the number of children. The percentages are

stated in ranges: 17%–23% (one child), 23%–28% (two children), 25%–32% (three children), 29%–35% (four children), and 31%–37% (five or more children). Deviation is permitted upon written findings explaining why the child support under the guidelines would be unjust or inappropriate (such as ages of the children; extraordinary medical costs; educational costs; day care costs; shared physical custody arrangements, including extended visitation; a party's other support obligations to another household). Support continues until the child reaches the age of majority, dies, marries, or becomes emancipated (can be extended to age 20 if the child is attending secondary school). Permits jury trials in contested cases.

Ga. Code Ann. Sec.19-6-17. Child support cannot be retroactively modified.

Ga. Code Ann. Sec. 19-6-19. Modification of weekly, monthly, annual, or similar periodic payments is permitted every three years or within two years upon showing a change in the income and financial status of the parent or needs of the child.

**Agency:**
Child Support Enforcement
Department of Human Resources
2 Peachtree Street
Suite 20445
Atlanta, GA 30303
404-657-3851
800-227-7993 (for 706 & 912 area codes)

**Website:**
http://ocse.dhr.georgia.gov

## HAWAII

**Law:**
Hawaii Revised Statutes Annotated. Haw. Rev. Stat. Ann. Sec. (Ignore volume numbers—look for "title" numbers.)

**Paternity:**
Haw. Rev. Stat. Ann. Sec. 584-4. A man is presumed to be the natural father of a child if: he and the child's natural mother are or have been married to each other and the child is born during the marriage, or within 300 days after the marriage is terminated by death, annulment, declaration of invalidity, or divorce, or after a decree of separation is entered by a court; before the child's birth, he and the child's natural mother have attempted to marry each other by an invalid marriage and the child is either born during the attempted marriage, or within 300 days after its termination by death, annulment, declaration of invalidity, or divorce or within 300 days after the termination of cohabitation; after the child's birth, he and the child's natural mother have married, or attempted to marry, each other (even if the attempted marriage is or could be declared invalid) and he has acknowledged his paternity of the child in writing filed with the department of health; with his consent, he is named as the child's father on the child's birth certificate; or he is obligated to support the child under a written voluntary promise or by court order; while the child is under the age of majority, he receives the child into his home and openly holds out the child as his natural child; he submits to court ordered DNA tests which show at least a 99% probability that he is the father of the child; or, he signs a voluntary, written acknowledgment of paternity of the child and files it with the department of health.

Haw. Rev. Stat. Ann. Sec. 584-3.5. Provides for voluntary acknowledgment of paternity. The acknowledgment must be signed by the mother and father and a witness. The signed voluntary acknowledgment of paternity shall constitute a legal finding of paternity, subject to the right of any signatory to rescind the acknowledgment within sixty days of signature or before the date of a proceeding relating to the child, including a proceeding to establish a support order to which the signatory is a party, whichever is sooner. After that period, an acknowledgment of paternity may be challenged in court only on the basis of fraud, duress, or material mistake of fact. The legal responsibilities of any party arising from the acknowledgment, including child support obligations, are not suspended during the challenge, except for good cause shown.

**Child Support:**
Hawaii Child Support Guidelines. Hawaii modified its guidelines in 2004. Gross income includes all forms of income, including self employment and lottery or gambling winnings, but does not include public assistance benefits. When a parent is employed at less than earning capacity, income may be imputed. Special calculations apply when parents have extensive visitation or parenting time. The new guidelines provide that child support should continue for full time students until age 23, with due consideration for the child's earnings and property. A court may order parents to contribute to the support of a disabled child beyond age 23.

**Modification:**
Either parent may seek a modification of a child support order every three years. In addition, at any time a material change in cir-cumstances can result in a request by either party to change child support. A material change in circumstances will be presumed if the new calculation is 10% greater or less than the current order.

**Agency:**
Child Support Enforcement Agency
Department of Attorney General
601 Kamokila Boulevard
Suite 251
Kakuhihewa State Office Building
Kapolei, HI 96707
808-692-8265 (Oahu)
888-317-9081 (Mainland)

**Website:**
www.hawaii.gov/ag/csea

# IDAHO

### Law:
Idaho Code. Idaho Code Sec. (Ignore volume numbers.)

### Paternity:
Idaho Code Sec. 7-1116. A man is presumed to be the father of a child born during marriage. An unmarried parent is liable for the support of his or her child. A court can determine paternity or the parties can acknowledge paternity.

Idaho Code Sec. 7-1106. A voluntary acknowledgment of paternity for an Idaho birth is admissible as evidence of paternity and constitutes a legal finding of paternity upon the filing of a signed and notarized acknowledgment with the vital statistics unit of the Department of Health and Welfare. An acknowledgment of paternity may be withdrawn by filing a notarized rescission with the vital statistics unit within the earlier of sixty days after the acknowledgment is filed or the date of an administrative or judicial proceeding relating to the child, including a proceeding to establish a support order, in which the signatory is a party. After that period, an executed acknowledgment of paternity may be challenged only in court on the basis of fraud, duress, or material mistake of fact. The legal responsibilities, including the obligation to pay child support, of any party to the acknowledgment is in effect, unless good cause is shown.

### Child Support:
Idaho Rules of Civil Procedure, Rule 6(c)(6). The guidelines are premised on the concept that both parents should support their children. The guidelines apply to children under 18 years of age or children pursuing high school education up to the age of 19. The guidelines are based on the gross income of the parents less permitted adjustments (such as alimony, maintenance, and other child support paid). Health care expenses and work-related child care

expenses may be added to the amount due. The total amount of child support would be divided between the parents as a proportion of their guideline incomes according to a schedule based on number of children and a sliding amount due per income bracket. For example, the schedule provides that for one child, 17% of the parents' combined guideline income of $10,000 is due, plus 15% of the next $20,000, 13% of the next $20,000, 10% of the next $20,000, etc. Adjustment to the guidelines are made in cases of shared physical custody (defined as more than 35% of the overnights in a year with each parent). For extended visits, the guidelines may also provide up to a 50% reduction of support for the duration of the actual physical custody in the visiting parent.

A substantial and material change of circumstances will support a motion for modification of child support obligations.

**Agency:**
Bureau of Child Support Services
Department of Health and Welfare
450 West State Street
5th Floor
P.O. Box 83720
Boise, ID 83720
208-334-5500
800-356-9868

**Website:**
www.healthandwelfare.idaho.gov

# ILLINOIS

**Law:**
Illinois Compiled Statutes. ILCS.

**Paternity:**
750 ILCS 45/5. A man is presumed to be the natural father of a child if: he and the child's natural mother are or have been married to each other, even though the marriage is or could be declared invalid, and the child is born or conceived during such marriage; after the child's birth, he and the child's natural mother have married each other, even though the marriage is or could be declared invalid, and he is named, with his written consent, as the child's father on the birth certificate; he and the child's natural mother have signed an acknowledgment of paternity; or, he and the child's natural mother have signed an acknowledgment of parentage.

750 ILCS 45/6. An acknowledgment of paternity must be signed by both parties and witnessed; it permits the father's name to be entered on the birth certificate. Paternity established by acknowledgment has the same effect as a judgment of paternity and is a basis for seeking a child support order without any further proceedings to establish paternity. A signed acknowledgment of paternity may be challenged in court only on the basis of fraud, duress, or material mistake of fact. Pending outcome of the challenge to the acknowledgment of paternity, the legal responsibilities of the signatories shall remain in full force and effect, except upon order of the court upon a showing of good cause.

750 ILCS 45/5. An acknowledgment may be withdrawn by a party upon the signing and witnessing of a form on the earlier of sixty days after the date the acknowledgment of parentage is signed, or the date of an administrative or judicial proceeding relating to the

child (including a proceeding to establish a support order) in which the signatory is a party, except that if a minor has signed the acknowledgment of paternity, the presumption becomes conclusive six months after the minor reaches majority or is otherwise emancipated.

**Child Support:**
750 ILCS 5/505. The court may order either or both parents owing a duty of support to a child of the marriage to pay an amount reasonable and necessary for his support, without regard to marital misconduct. The duty of support owed to a minor child includes the obligation to provide for the reasonable and necessary physical, mental, and emotional health needs of the child. The guidelines are based on a percentage of the noncustodial parent's income: 20% (one child), 28% (two children), 32% (three children), 40% (four children), 45% (five children), and 50% (six or more children).

Departures from the guidelines may be based on: the financial resources and needs of the child; the financial resources and needs of the custodial parent; the standard of living the child would have enjoyed had the marriage not been dissolved; the physical and emotional condition of the child, and his educational needs; and, the financial resources and needs of the noncustodial parent.

An order for support must include a date on which child support terminates. The date can be no earlier than the child turns age 18 or is otherwise emancipated. The termination date does not apply to any unpaid support owed.

Each payment due under a support order is considered an enforceable judgment against the person obligated to pay. A lien arises by operation of law against the real and personal property of the noncustodial parent for each installment of overdue support owed by the noncustodial parent.

Modification may be requested only as to installments accruing subsequent to due notice by the moving party of the filing of the motion for modification. An order for child support may be modified upon a showing of a substantial change in circumstances and without the necessity of showing a substantial change in circumstances, upon a showing of an inconsistency of at least 20%, but no less than $10 per month, between the amount of the existing order and the amount of child support that results from application of the guidelines.

**Agency:**
Division of Child Support Enforcement
Illinois Department of Public Aid
509 South Sixth Street
6ᵗʰ Floor
Springfield, IL 62701
217-782-1820
800-447-4278 (in-state only)
877-225-7077 (payments)

**Website:**
www.ilchildsupport.com

## INDIANA

**Law:**
Indiana Code Annotated. Ind. Code Ann. Sec. (Look for "title" numbers.)

**Paternity:**
Ind. Code Ann. Sec. 31-14-1. A man is presumed to be the natural father of a child if: he and the child's natural mother are or have been married to each other (even if the marriage is invalid) and the child is born during, or within 300 days of, the marriage; or a DNA test shows the man has a 99% probability of being the child's father.

Ind. Code Ann. Sec. 16-37-2-2.1. The parties may sign an acknowledgment of paternity, called an *affidavit of paternity*. The mother has sole legal custody as a result of the signing unless a court orders otherwise. An acknowledgment of paternity may not be withdrawn more than sixty days after signing unless a court finds that there has been fraud, duress, or a material mistake in signing the acknowledgment. Unless good cause is shown, a court will not order child support during a challenge to the affidavit. A mother who knowingly or intentionally falsely names a man as the father commits a Class A Misdemeanor.

**Child Support:**
Indiana Child Support Guidelines (Supreme Court Order). New guidelines were adopted in 2004. The guidelines state that the gross income of both parents is added together after certain adjustments are made, and a percentage share of income for each parent is determined. Then applying the support tables, the total cost of supporting a child or children is determined. Work-related child care expenses and health insurance premiums for the child(ren) are then added to the basic child support obligation. The child support obligation is then prorated between the parents, based on their proportionate share of the adjusted income. If a judge believes that in a

particular case application of the Guideline amount would be unreasonable, unjust, or inappropriate, a finding must be made that sets forth the reason for deviating from the guidelines (such as union dues owed, support for an elderly parent, purchase of school clothes, extraordinary medical expenses, and long-distance travel).

**Agency:**
Child Support Bureau
Division of Family and Children
402 West Washington Street
Room W360
Indianapolis, IN 46204
317-232-4885
800-840-8757

**Website:**
www.in.gov/dcs/support

## IOWA

**Law:**
Iowa Code Annotated. Iowa Code Ann. Sec. (Ignore volume numbers; look for "section" numbers.)

**Paternity:**
Iowa Code Ann. Sec. 252A.3. A man is presumed to be the father of a child born at any time prior or subsequent to marriage, regardless of the validity of such marriage. Persons, though not married, who hold themselves out as husband and wife by virtue of a common law marriage, are deemed the legal parents of their children. The paternity of a child born outside marriage is determined by order of court or by acknowledgment of the parents.

Iowa Code Ann. Sec. 252A.3A. An acknowledgment of paternity of a child, which is called an affidavit of paternity, consists of: a statement by the mother agreeing to the father's statement of paternity and the identity of the father, and acknowledging either that the mother was unmarried at the time of conception, birth, and at any time during the period between conception and birth of the child, or that the mother was married at the time of conception, birth, or at any time during the period between conception and birth of the child, and that a court order has been entered ruling that the individual to whom the mother was married at that time is not the father of the child; and, a statement from the putative father that the putative father is the father of the child. The affidavit must be signed by both parents and notarized. An affidavit of paternity that is filed with the state registrar is admissible as evidence of paternity and has the same legal effect as a judgment of paternity. It also serves as a basis for seeking child or medical support without further determination of paternity.

A completed affidavit of paternity may be withdrawn by filing with the state registrar a completed and notarized rescission form signed by either the mother or putative father who signed the affidavit of paternity that the putative father is not the father of the child. The recission form must be filed prior to the earliest of the following: sixty days after the latest notarized signature of the mother or putative father on the affidavit of paternity, or entry of a court order pursuant to a proceeding in this state to which the signatory is a party relating to the child, including a proceeding to establish a support order.

**Child Support:**
Iowa Child Support Guidelines. The guideline schedules are based on net income of the noncustodial parent (gross income less deductions, such as taxes withheld, Social Security deductions, mandatory pension deductions, union dues, health insurance premiums deducted from wages, prior child and spouse support paid pursuant to court or administrative order, and certain child care expenses). Parties may enter into an agreement for child support and medical support if the amount is in substantial compliance with the guidelines. If not, the court must determine whether it is justified and appropriate; and, if so, include the stated reasons for the variance in the order. The guidelines amount may be adjusted upward or downward if the court finds it is necessary to do so to provide for the needs of the children and to do justice between the parties under the special circumstances of the case.

**Agency:**
Bureau of Collections
Department of Human Services
400 SW 8th Street
Suite M
Des Moines, IA 50309
515-242-5530
888-229-9223

**Website:**
www.dhs.state.ia.us

# KANSAS

## Law:
Kansas Statutes Annotated. Kan. Stat. Ann. Sec. These can also be *Vernon's* Kansas Statutes Annotated.

## Paternity:
Kan. Stat. Ann. Sec. 38-1114. A man is presumed to be the father of a child if: the man and the child's mother are, or have been, married to each other and the child is born during the marriage or within 300 days after the marriage is terminated by death or by the filing of a journal entry of a decree of annulment or divorce; before the child's birth, the man and the child's mother have attempted to marry each other (even though the marriage is invalid) and the child is born during the attempted marriage or within 300 days after the parties' cohabitation or the termination of the attempted marriage; after the child's birth, the man and the child's mother have married, or attempted to marry (even though the marriage is invalid) and the man has acknowledged paternity of the child in writing, with the man's consent, the man is named as the child's father on the child's birth certificate, or the man is obligated to support the child under a written voluntary promise or by a court order; the man by his conduct or in writing recognizes paternity of the child; the man completes a voluntary acknowledgment in accordance with Kan. Stat. Ann. Secs. 38-1130 or 65-2409a.; or, DNA tests indicate at least a 97% probability that the man is the father of the child.

Kan. Stat. Ann. Sec. 38-1113. The parentage of the child may be established by a voluntary acknowledgment or by judgment. Under Kan. Stat. Ann. Sec. 38-1138 the voluntary acknowledgment creates a permanent father-child relationship unless vacated by court order. Pursuant to Kan. Stat. Ann. Sec. 38-1115 an acknowledgment can be withdrawn within sixty days or before any court hearing related to the child, whichever is earlier. After that period, the father must show fraud, duress, or an important mistake of fact. The legal responsibilities, including any child support obligation, of any signatory arising from the acknowledgment of paternity shall not be suspended during the challenge to the acknowledgment, except for good cause shown. Any request to withdraw must be filed in court within one year unless the father was under age 18 when he acknowledged paternity. In such a case, he has one year after he turns age 18 to file. If the child is more than one year old when the request to withdraw acknowledgment is filed, the court will first consider the best interests of the child.

## Child Support:

Kansas Administrative Order No. 128. New guidelines were adopted in 2004 to increase support orders by 3% from the previous schedule. A court may order child support and education expenses to be paid by either or both parents for any child up to 18 years of age (19 if still in high school) unless the parents agree in writing, which is approved by the court, to pay support beyond the time the child reaches 18 years of age. In determining the amount, the court will consider all relevant factors, without regard to marital misconduct, including the financial resources and needs of both parents, the financial resources and needs of the child and the physical and emotional condition of the child. Until a child reaches 18 years of age, the court may set apart any portion of property of either the husband or wife, or both, for the support of the child. The schedules are based on the parents' combined income, the number of children in the family, and the ages of the children. The guideline schedules allow for certain deductions from gross income and special schedules apply to shared and divided custody cases. Every order requiring payment of child support shall require that the support be paid through the clerk of the district court or the court trustee except for good cause shown. The court may make a modification of child support retroactive to a date at least one month after the date that the motion to modify was filed with the court.

A court may order a modification on request when there is a material change in circumstance, which includes a change in financial circumstances of the parents or the guidelines, which would increase or decrease by 10% or more the child support obligation, the 7th and 16th birthdays of the child, and emancipation of a child.

**Agency:**
Child Support Enforcement Program
Department of Social & Rehabilitation Services
P.O. Box 497
Topeka, KS 66601
785-296-3237
800-432-0152 (for withholding)
877-572-5722 (for collections)
800-432-3913 (for reporting fraud)

**Website:**
www.srskansas.org/services/cse/cse.htm

# KENTUCKY

### Law:

Kentucky Revised Statutes Annotated. Ky. Rev. Stat. Ann. Sec. (Ignore volume numbers—look for "chapter" numbers.)

### Paternity:

Ky. Rev. Stat. Ann. Sec. 406.011. The father of a child that is or may be born outside of marriage is liable to the same extent as the father of a child born in marriage for the support of his child. A child born during marriage or within ten months thereafter, is presumed to be the child of the husband and wife. A court may establish paternity or the parties may acknowledge paternity.

Ky. Rev. Stat. Ann. Sec. 406.025. Provides that a voluntary acknowledgment of paternity creates a rebuttable presumption of paternity. The acknowledgment, called an affidavit, must be signed by the mother and father, notarized, and submitted to the state registrar of vital statistics. Upon filing, paternity shall be rebuttably presumed for the earlier of sixty days or the date of an administrative or judicial proceeding relating to the child, including a proceeding to establish a child support order. Unless good cause is shown, court or administratively ordered child support continues until final judicial or administrative determination of paternity.

### Child Support:

Ky. Rev. Stat. Ann. Sec. 403-211-212. The child support guidelines are a rebuttable presumption for the establishment of the amount of child support. A court may deviate from the guidelines where their application would be unjust or inappropriate. Any deviation shall be accompanied by a written finding or specific finding on the record by the court, specifying the reason for the deviation. Reasons for a deviation include: a child's extraordinary medical, dental, educational, job training, or special needs; either parent's own extraordinary needs, such as medical expenses; the independent financial resources, if any, of the child or children; and, that the parents of the child have agreed to child support different from the guideline amount.

To determine the amount of child support, Kentucky uses a worksheet based on the guidelines. The worksheet uses the income of both parents and considers other factors such as medical insurance, maintenance payments, child care, and prior child support owed.

Modifications are permitted under Sec. 403.213 upon a showing of a material change in circumstances that is substantial and continuing such as where, for example, the obligation reflects at least a 15% change in the order. Child support may be modified only as to installments accruing after the filing of the motion for modification.

**Agency:**
Division of Child Support Enforcement
Cabinet for Human Resources
P.O. Box 2150
Frankfort, KY 40602
502-564-2285
800-248-1163

**Website:**
www.chfs.ky.gov/dcbs/dcs

# LOUISIANA

## Law:
*West's* Louisiana Revised Statutes Annotated. La. Rev. Stat. Ann. Sec. AND *West's* Louisiana Civil Code Annotated. La. Civ. Code Ann. art.

## Paternity:
La. Civ. Code art. 184. The husband of the mother is presumed to be the father of a child born or conceived during the marriage.

La. Civ. Code art. 185. A child born less than 300 days after the dissolution of the marriage is presumed to have been conceived during the marriage. A child born 300 days or more after the dissolution of the marriage is not presumed to be the child of the husband.

La. Civ. Code art. 198. Illegitimate children are legitimated by the subsequent marriage of their father and mother, whenever the parents have acknowledged them as their children, either before or after the marriage.

La. Civ. Code art. 203. The acknowledgment of an illegitimate child shall be made by a declaration executed before a notary public, in the presence of two witnesses, by the father and mother or either of them, or it may be made in the registering of the birth or baptism of such child. Such an acknowledgment is a legal finding of paternity and is sufficient to establish child support without the necessity of obtaining a judgment of paternity. Under La. Civ. Code art. 205, a father may complete an acknowledgment independently.

La. Civ. Code art. 206. An acknowledgment may be withdrawn before the earlier of sixty days of the signing of the acknowledgment in a judicial hearing for the limited purpose of rescinding the acknowledgment or declaration or in a judicial hearing relating to the child, including a child support proceeding, wherein the challenger is a party to the proceeding. At any time, a person who signed the acknowledgment may petition the court to void such acknowledgment but only upon proof, by clear and convincing evidence, that such act was induced by fraud, duress, or material mistake of fact, or that the person is not the biological parent of the child. Except for good cause shown, the court will not suspend any legal responsibilities or obligations, including a support obligation, of the person during the pendency of the challenge.

**Child Support:**
La. Rev. Stat. Ann Secs. 9:315–9:315.14. The premise of the guidelines is that child support is a continuous obligation of both parents, children are entitled to share in the current income of both parents, and children should not be the economic victims of divorce or out-of-marriage birth. The guidelines are based on the combined gross income of the parents less preexisting orders for child or spousal support. A court may deviate from the guidelines if their application would not be in the best interest of the child or would be inequitable to the parties (such as for certain extraordinary medical expenses or extraordinary community debt of the parties). Parties may agree to support, but a court may require proof of income. Calculation of support is based on the proportionate percentage of the combined amount of adjusted gross income. Next, the basic child support obligation amount is determined from the schedule in La. Rev. Stat. Ann. Sec. 9:315.14 by using the combined adjusted gross income of the parties and the number of children. Finally, the amount due is adjusted to include health insurance and certain child care costs, education, or transportation costs. Each parent's share of child support is then determined by multiplying his or her percentage share of combined adjusted gross income times the total child support obligation. The party without legal custody owes his or her total child support obligation as a money judgment of child support to the custodial parent, minus any court-ordered direct payments made on behalf of the child for work-related net child

care costs, health insurance premiums, extraordinary medical expenses, or extraordinary expenses provided as adjustments to the schedule. There are special considerations in cases of joint custody.

La. Rev. Stat. Ann. Secs. 9:315.11, 14. Modification is permitted upon proof of a material change in circumstances of one of the parties between the time of the previous award and the time of the motion for modification of the award. Modification of child support is permitted back to the date of the filing of the request.

**Agency:**
Support Enforcement Services
Office of Family Support
P.O. Box 94065
Baton Rouge, LA 70804
225-342-4780
800-256-4650 (in-state only)

**Website:**
www.dss.state.la.us/departments/ofs/support_enforcement_
      services.html

# MAINE

## Law:
Maine Revised Statutes Annotated. Me. Rev. Stat. Ann. tit. Sec.

## Paternity:
Me. Rev. Stat. Ann. tit. 1 Sec. 1552. The father of a child who is or may be born outside of marriage is liable to the same extent as the father of a child born in marriage for the support of his child. Paternity may be determined upon the filing of a complaint or by acknowledgment.

Me. Rev. Stat. Ann. tit. 19-A Sec. 1616. A signed voluntary acknowledgment of paternity is a legal finding of paternity, subject to the right of a signatory to rescind the acknowledgment within the earlier of sixty days or the date of an administrative or judicial proceeding relating to the child, including a proceeding to establish a support order, in which the signatory is a party. After the right to rescind ends, the acknowledgment may be challenged in court only on the basis of fraud, duress, or material mistake of fact. The legal responsibilities of a signatory arising from the acknowledgment, including child support obligations, may not be suspended during the challenge except for good cause shown.

## Child Support:
Me. Rev. Stat. Ann. tit. 19-A, Secs. 2001–2010. There is a rebuttable presumption that the child support amount as calculated from the support guidelines is the amount ordered to be paid. The parties can make an agreement on the amount of the child support obligation, but the court or hearing officer will review the adequacy of a child support amount agreed to by the parties. A deviation from the guideline is permitted if the court or hearing officer finds that a child support order based on the support guidelines would be inequitable or unjust as defined in Sec. 2007.

This is a combined income state which means that the parties' annual gross income is added together then applied to the guideline for adjustment. The basic support amount is determined by adding together the annual gross income of both parties, and referring to the child support table for the amount based on the number of children to be supported. To this will be added child care costs and extraordinary medical expenses. Then, the total support obligation is divided between the parties in proportion based on their respective gross incomes. The parent not providing primary residential care will pay their share of support to the parent providing primary residential care; it is presumed that the parent providing residential care will pay their share directly for the child's support. There are special calculations for shared custody. Child support will be provided until the child turns age 18 (19 if the child is in secondary school), gets married, or joins the armed services. The order may include automatic adjustments to the amount of money paid for the support of a child when the child attains 12 or 18 years of age; or when the child graduates, withdraws or is expelled from secondary school, attains 19 years of age, or is otherwise emancipated.

Modification is permitted upon request and proof of a substantial change of circumstances, such as where a child support order varies more than 15% from the guidelines amount, except where the deviation was permitted at the initial order. If it has been three years or longer since the order was issued or modified, the court or hearing officer will review the order without requiring proof or showing of a change of circumstances.

Child support orders may be modified retroactively, but only from the date that notice of a petition for modification has been served upon the opposing party, pursuant to the Maine Rules of Civil Procedure.

**Agency:**
Division of Support Enforcement and Recovery
Bureau of Family Independence
Department of Human Services
State House Station 11
268 Whitten Road
Augusta ME 04333
207-287-2886
800-371-3101 (in-state only)

**Website:**
www.maine.gov/dhhs/bcfs

## MARYLAND

**Law:**
Annotated Code of Maryland, Family Code. Md. Fam. Law Code Ann. Sec.

**Paternity:**
Md. Fam. Law Code Ann. Sec. 5-1005. A man is presumed to be the father of a child born to the parties during marriage. A child born to parents who are not married is considered to be the child of his father only if the father: has been judicially determined to be the father in an action brought under the statutes relating to paternity proceedings; has acknowledged himself, in writing, to be the father; has openly and notoriously recognized the child to be his child; or, has subsequently married the mother and has acknowledged himself, orally or in writing, to be the father.

Md. Fam. Law Code Ann. Sec. 5-1028. Parents may execute a voluntary acknowledgment of paternity, called an affidavit of parentage, which constitutes a legal finding of paternity. The signatures of both parties must attest, under penalty of perjury, that the information provided on the affidavit is true and correct. Either parent may withdraw his or her acknowledgment within sixty days or the filing of a proceeding relating to the child, whichever comes first. After the expiration of the sixty-day period, an executed affidavit of parentage may be challenged in court only on the basis of fraud, duress, or material mistake of fact. The legal responsibilities of any signatory arising from the affidavit, including child support, will not be suspended during the challenge, except for good cause shown.

**Child Support:**
Md. Fam. Law Code Ann. Sec. 12-201-204. There is a rebuttable presumption that the amount of child support that would result

from the application of the child support guidelines set forth in this subtitle is the correct amount of child support to be awarded. The presumption may be rebutted by evidence that the application of the guidelines would be unjust or inappropriate in a particular case. For example, deviation from the guidelines is permitted if the court determines that application of the guidelines in a particular case would be inappropriate (such as contributions to other children).

The guidelines are based on a percentage of both parents' combined actual income less adjustments for child support obligations and alimony actually paid, and the cost of health insurance for the child(ren). Basic child support is determined by applying the combined adjusted actual income to a schedule of amounts based on the number of children to be supported. Adjustments are made to account for child care expenses, extraordinary medical expenses, and the cost of special or private education and transportation between the homes of the parents. For sole physical custody cases, the total child support amount is divided between the parents according to their percentage share of the combined income. The amount owed by the custodial parent is presumed to be spent on the child. The amount owed by the noncustodial parent becomes the child support order. In a shared physical custody arrangement, additional adjustments are made to the support obligation amount to reflect the extra expenses incurred in such an arrangement and to account for the percentage of time the child spends overnight with each parent. The respective child support obligation amounts owed by each parent are offset against each other and the parent owing the greater amount would owe the difference to the other parent as child support. Md. Fam. Law Code Ann. Sec. 12-202. Request for modification will be permitted upon a showing of a material or substantial change in the circumstances surrounding the parties. However, child support may not be retroactively modified except to the period covering the filing of a petition for modification.

**Agency:**
Child Support Enforcement Administration
Department of Human Resources
311 West Saratoga Street
Baltimore, MD 21201
410-767-7934
800-332-6347

**Website:**
www.dhr.state.md.us/csea

# MASSACHUSETTS

**Law:**
Annotated Laws of Massachusetts. Mass. Gen. Laws. Ann. ch. Sec.

**Paternity:**
Mass. Gen. Laws Ann. ch. 209C, Sec. 6. A man is presumed to be the father of a child if: he and the mother of the child are married to each other (even if the marriage is invalid) and the child is born during the marriage or within 300 days after the marriage is terminated; after the birth of the child, he and the mother of the child married each other (even if the marriage is declared invalid) and he voluntarily agreed to paternity or engaged in conduct that showed he acknowledged paternity; he is named as the child's father on the child's birth certificate with consent of the mother; while the child was under the age of majority, he and the mother took the child into their home and openly held out the child as theirs; or, he acknowledged paternity in a parental responsibility claim and the mother failed to object after notice.

Mass. Gen. Laws Ann. ch. 209C, Sec. 2. Paternity may be established by filing a signed and notarized acknowledgment of parentage. The acknowledgment must be signed by both parents (whether minors or not) or by filing a court case to establish paternity. An acknowledgment, when filed with the registrar of vital records and statistics or with the court, will be sufficient to obtain custody and support.

Mass. Gen. Laws Ann. ch. 209C, Sec. 11(a). An acknowledgment may be withdrawn within sixty days of signing by filing a case and notifying the other parent. After that time, the person seeking to withdraw has one year to file a case in which he or she must prove fraud, duress, or material mistake of fact. A timely filed challenge will result in the court ordering a DNA test. The responsibilities of a party who signed an acknowledgment will not be suspended during the challenge unless the court so orders for good cause shown.

**Child Support:**

Massachusetts Child Support Guidelines. Massachusett's guidelines are undergoing a review in 2006. The goals of the guidelines include: to minimize the economic impact on the child of family breakup, and to encourage joint parental responsibility for child support in proportion to, or as a percentage of, income. A 2005 change in the law means that there is a presumption that the guidelines apply in all cases seeking the establishment of a child support order. A specific, written finding that the guidelines would be unjust or inappropriate and that the best interests of the child have been considered in a particular case will permit deviation from the guidelines.

The guidelines are based on gross income. Added adjustments are made based on health care expenses and age of the child. The guidelines use a sliding percentage of income basis (plus or minus 2%) based on number of children. Special calculations apply to shared or split custody and extended visitation cases.

A modification may be allowed if there is at least a 20% difference between a support order and one calculated under the guidelines.

**Agency:**

Child Support Enforcement Division
Department of Revenue
P.O. Box 9561
Boston, MA 02114-9561
800-332-2733

**Website:**

www.cse.state.ma.us

# MICHIGAN

**Law:**
Michigan Compiled Laws Annotated. Mich. Comp. Laws. Ann. Sec.

**Paternity:**
Mich. Comp. Laws. Ann. Sec. 552.29. A man is presumed to be the father of a child born during marriage. Under Mich. Comp. Laws. Ann. Sec. 722.712, both parents of a child born out of wedlock are liable for the necessary support and education of the child. Paternity may be established by filing an action to determine paternity or where the child's father acknowledges paternity.

Mich. Comp. Laws. Ann. Sec. 722.1001-1013. An acknowledgment of parentage is valid and effective if signed by the mother and father whose signatures are notarized. An acknowledgment may be signed any time during the child's lifetime. A minor parent may sign an acknowledgment of parentage with the same effect as if he or she were of legal age. After a mother and father sign an acknowledgment of parentage, the mother is presumed to have custody of the minor child unless otherwise determined by the court or otherwise agreed upon by the parties in writing.

Mich. Comp. Laws. Ann. Sec. 722.1011. The parents, child, or a prosecuting attorney may file a claim for revocation of an acknowledgment of parentage. A claim for revocation must be accompanied by an affidavit signed by the claimant setting forth at least one of the following reasons: mistake of fact; newly discovered evidence that by due diligence could not have been found before the acknowledgment was signed; fraud; misrepresentation or misconduct; or duress in signing the acknowledgment. A court can order DNA tests in the proceeding.

214 • Child Support Made Easy

**Child Support:**

Mich. Child Support Guidelines. In December 2003, the Michigan Supreme Court directed certain changes to the guidelines that took effect in October 2004, including changes related to (1) determining medical support and health care coverage options, (2) setting child support before determining spousal support, and (3) deviations. The guidelines are presumed to be the correct calculation for a child support order. The parties may agree to a deviation, or the court may enter an order that deviates from the formula if the court determines from the facts of the case that application of the child support formula would be unjust or inappropriate.

Michigan guidelines use an Income Shares Model, which considers both parents' relative incomes in the calculation of support. The state updates the income brackets of its guidelines formula annually. The guidelines address several dozen factors that affect the straight application of the base child support formula. For example, there are formulaic adjustments for child care, the child's medical expenses, extended visitation, shared-parenting time, and others. The guidelines are based on the net income of each party which is then adjusted for the presence of other children in the home or prior support orders. Then the custodial parent's income is compared to the noncustodial parent's income on a table based on the number of children to determine the guideline amount due. A court may order child support for the time a child is regularly attending high school on a full-time basis with a reasonable expectation of completing sufficient credits to graduate from high school while residing on a full-time basis with the recipient of support or at an institution, until the child reaches 19 years and 6 months of age.

Periodically, the Michigan friend of the court office will review child support orders to determine whether the difference between the recommended amount and the current order is more than 10% or $25, whichever is less. Note that this could increase or decrease the order.

If the proposed change meets that threshold amount, the court office must petition to modify the order.

A court may also modify an order of child support, as the circumstances of the parents and the benefit of the children require. All relevant factors are to be considered in determining whether there has been a change of circumstances sufficient to justify a modification of an order granting child support. Retroactive modification of a support payment due under a support order is permitted to relate back to the filing of a petition for modification, but only from the date that notice of the petition was given to the payer or recipient of support.

**Agency:**
Office of Child Support
Family Independence Agency
P.O. Box 30478
Lansing, MI 48909

*Street Address:*
325 South Grand Avenue
Lansing, MI 48909
517-241-7460

**Website:**
www.michigan.gov/dhs

## MINNESOTA

**Law:**
Minnesota Statutes Annotated. Minn. Stat. Ann. Sec.

**Paternity:**
Minn. Stat. Ann. Sec. 257.55. A man is presumed to be the biological father of a child if: (a) he and the child's biological mother are or have been married to each other and the child is born during the marriage, or within 280 days after the marriage is terminated by death, annulment, declaration of invalidity, dissolution, or divorce, or after a decree of legal separation is entered by a court; (b) before the child's birth, he and the child's biological mother have attempted to marry each other by a marriage solemnized in apparent compliance with law, although the attempted marriage is or could be declared void, voidable, or otherwise invalid, and, (1) if the attempted marriage could be declared invalid only by a court, the child is born during the attempted marriage, or within 280 days after its termination by death, annulment, declaration of invalidity, dissolution or divorce, or (2) if the attempted marriage is invalid without a court order, the child is born within 280 days after the termination of cohabitation; (c) after the child's birth, he and the child's biological mother have married, or attempted to marry, each other by a marriage solemnized in apparent compliance with law, although the attempted marriage is or could be declared void, voidable, or otherwise invalid, and, (1) he has acknowledged his paternity of the child in writing filed with the state registrar of vital statistics, (2) with his consent, he is named as the child's father on the child's birth record, or (3) he is obligated to support the child under a written voluntary promise or by court order; (d) while the child is under the age of majority, he receives the child into his home and openly holds out the child as his biological child; (e) he and the child's biological mother acknowledge his paternity of the child in a writing signed by both of them under section 257.34 and filed with the state

registrar of vital statistics; or, (f) DNA evidence establishes at least a 99% likelihood that he is the father of the child.

Minn. Stat. Ann. Sec. 257.75. The statute establishes a procedure for executing and withdrawing an acknowledgment, called a recognition of parentage. A recognition of parentage may be signed by an adult or minor and notarized. The recognition of parentage creates a presumption of paternity. Either parent may seek to withdraw the recognition of parentage by filing an action within the earlier of sixty days after the recognition is executed or the date of a hearing relating to the child. If no challenge is made to the recognition, the recognition has the force and effect of a judgment or order determining the existence of the parent and child relationship.

An action to vacate a recognition of paternity must be brought within one year or within six months of the results of a DNA test. A child has six months after obtaining the result of DNA tests that indicate that the man who signed the recognition is not the father of the child, or within one year of reaching the age of majority, whichever is later. The challenger must prove fraud, duress, or material mistake of fact. The legal responsibilities in existence at the time of an action to vacate, including child support obligations, may not be suspended during the proceeding, except for good cause shown.

**Child Support:**
Minn. Stat. Ann. Secs. 518 (recodified as amended by S.F. 630). Minnesota made major changes in its guidelines which are effective January 1, 2007. It changed from a percentage of income state to an income shares model. Under the new model, the basic child support obligation is determined by combining parental income using a support table. Parties can request a review hearing on a written request six months after a judgment of dissolution, legal separation or child custody, parenting time, or child support order. The new guidelines grant

parents a parenting-time adjustment of 12% if the child spends between 10% and 45% of time with them.

**Modification:**

During 2007, modification requests must show at least a 20% change in the gross income of the paying parent; a change in the number of children covered; a newly disabled child; or, an agreement by both parents to modify the existing order using the new guidelines. Modification of support may be made retroactive only with respect to the date of service of notice of the motion for modification. In 2008, Minnesota will replace the modification rules with new criteria.

**Agency:**
Child Support Enforcement Division
Department of Human Services
444 Lafayette Road
4th Floor
St. Paul, MN 55155
800-575-3954

**Website:**
www.dhs.state.mn.us

# MISSISSIPPI

## Law:
Mississippi Code Annotated. Miss. Code Ann. Sec.

## Paternity:
A man is presumed to be the father of a child if married to the mother at the time of the child's birth. An illegitimate child shall become a legitimate child of the natural father if the natural father marries the natural mother and acknowledges the child.

Miss. Code Ann. Sec. 93-9-7. The father of a child that is or may be born out of matrimony is liable to the same extent as the father of a child born of lawful matrimony, for the support of his child.

Miss. Code Ann. Sec. 93-9-9. Paternity may be established by a petition filed in a proceeding or by acknowledgment.

Miss. Code Ann. Secs. 93-9-9; 93-9-28. A signed voluntary acknowledgment of paternity is subject to the right of any signatory to rescind the acknowledgment within the earlier of sixty days, or the date of a judicial proceeding relating to the child, including a proceeding to establish a support order, in which the parent is a party. After that period, an acknowledgment of paternity may be challenged in court only on the basis of fraud, duress, or material mistake of fact. The legal responsibilities, including child support obligations, of any signatory arising from the acknowledgment may not be suspended during the pendency of the challenge, except for good cause shown.

## Child Support:
Miss Code Ann. Secs. 43-19-101–43-19-103. The child support guidelines are presumed to be correct in child support awards. Deviations are permitted upon a finding that the application of the

guidelines would be unjust or inappropriate in a particular case, such as, for example, where there are extraordinary medical, psychological, educational, or dental expenses.

The guidelines are based on a percentage of adjusted gross income of the noncustodial parent. Adjusted gross income equals gross income less deductions for taxes, social security, certain retirement contributions, and prior court-ordered amounts of child support. The percentages are 14% (one child), 20% (two children), 22% (three children), 24% (four children), and 26% (five or more children).

Modification is permitted upon a material change of circumstances of the father, mother, or child which arises after the original order. The effective date of a modification of child support payments is the date of the petition to modify.

**Agency:**
Division of Child Support
Department of Human Services
P.O. Box 352
Jackson, MS 39205
601-359-4861
800-434-5437 (Jackson)
800-354-6039 (Hines, Rankin, and Madison Counties)

**Website:**
www.mdhs.state.ms.us/cse.html

# MISSOURI

**Law:**
*Vernon's* Annotated Missouri Statutes. Mo. Rev. Stat. Sec.

**Paternity:**
Mo. Rev. Stat. Sec. 210.822. A man is presumed to be the natural father of a child if: (1) he and the child's natural mother are or have been married to each other and the child is born during the marriage, or within 300 days after the marriage is terminated; or (2) before the child's birth, he and the child's natural mother have attempted to marry each other by a marriage solemnized in apparent compliance with the law, although the attempted marriage is or may be declared invalid, and (a) if the attempted marriage may be declared invalid only by a court, the child is born during the attempted marriage or within three hundred days after its termination by death, annulment, declaration of invalidity or dissolution, or (b) if the marriage is invalid without a court order, the child is born within three hundred days after the termination of cohabitation; (3) after the child's birth, he and the child's natural mother have married or attempted to marry each other by a marriage solemnized in apparent compliance with law, although the marriage is or may be declared invalid, and (a) he has acknowledged his paternity of the child in writing filed with the bureau, or (b) with his consent, he is named as the child's father on the child's birth certificate, or (c) he is obligated to support the child pursuant to a written voluntary promise or by court order; or, (4) an expert concludes that the blood tests show that the alleged parent is not excluded and that the probability of paternity is 98%.

Mo. Rev. Stat. Secs. 193.087; 193.215. Paternity can be established where both parents sign an acknowledgment.

Mo. Rev. Stat. Sec. 210.823 provides that a signed acknowledgment of paternity is considered a legal finding of paternity. A parent who signed the acknowledgment may withdraw it in writing by filing a rescission within the earlier of sixty days from the date of the last signature or the date of an administrative or judicial proceeding to establish a support order in which the signatory is a party. After this period, the acknowledgment may only be challenged in court on the basis of fraud, duress, or material mistake of fact. Except for good cause shown, the legal responsibilities of the parties, including child support obligations, shall not be suspended during the pendency of any action in which an attempt is made to revoke the signed acknowledgment under this section.

**Child Support:**
Missouri Supreme Court Rule 88.01, Civil Procedure Form 14. There is a rebuttable presumption that the amount of child support calculated pursuant to Civil Procedure Form 14 is the correct amount of child support to be awarded in any judicial or administrative proceeding. A deviation to the guidelines is permitted upon a finding that the child support amount under a correctly calculated Form 14 would be unjust or inappropriate.

The guidelines are based on gross income for each parent less deductions for prior support orders. The total percentage due of combined income of each parent is then determined from the support chart. Work-related child care, medical costs, and other extraordinary costs are then added to the basic child support amount. Each parent's percentage of the obligation due is then determined (with credit for times of temporary physical custody).

Modification of child support is permitted upon a showing of changed circumstances so substantial and continuing as to make the terms of the existing order unreasonable. The court, in determining whether or not a substantial change in circumstances has occurred, will consider all financial resources of both parties, including the extent to which the reasonable expenses of either party are, or should be, shared by a spouse or other person with whom he or she cohabits, and the earning capacity of a party who is not employed. If the application of the child support guidelines to the financial circumstances of the parties would result in a change of child support from the existing amount by 20% or more, a *prima facie* showing has been made of a change of circumstances.

**Agency:**
Department of Social Services
Division of Child Support Enforcement
P.O. Box 2320
Jefferson City, MO 65102
573-751-4301
800-859-7999

**Website:**
www.dss.mo.gov

## MONTANA

**Law:**
Montana Code Annotated. Mont. Code Ann. Sec.

**Paternity:**
Mont. Code Ann. Sec. 40-6-105. (1) A man is presumed to be the natural father of a child if (a) he and the child's mother are or have been married and the child is born during the marriage or within 300 days after the marriage is terminated; (b) before the child's birth, the person and the child's natural mother have attempted to marry (even though the attempted marriage is invalid) and the child is born during the attempted marriage or within 300 days after its termination or the termination of cohabitation; (c) after the child's birth, he and the child's mother married or attempted to marry (even though the attempted marriage is invalid) and (i) the child's mother and father have acknowledged the alleged father's paternity that is filed with the department of public health and human services, (ii) he consents to be named as the child's father on the child's birth certificate, or (iii) he is obligated to support the child under a written voluntary promise or by court order; (d) while the child is under the age of majority, he receives the child into his home and openly represents the child to be his natural child; (e) he and the child's mother acknowledge his paternity of the child in a paternity acknowledgment form that is provided by the department of public health and human services; DNA tests show a 95% or higher probability of paternity; or (g) he is presumed to be the child's natural father under the laws of the state or Indian territory in which the child was born.

Mont. Code Ann. Sec. 40-6-105. An acknowledgment signed by the child's mother and father on a form that is provided by the department of public health and human services is binding on a parent who executes it, whether or not the parent is a minor. An acknowledgment of paternity under subsection may be rescinded by a signatory at any time within sixty days after it was signed by filing a notice of withdrawal with the department of public health and human services. The notice of withdrawal must include an affidavit attesting that a copy of the notice was provided to any parent who signed the acknowledgment form. After that period, the acknowledgment may only be set aside for fraud, duress, or material mistake of fact. Except for good cause, legal responsibilities arising from the paternity acknowledgment may not be stayed pending the outcome of an action to set aside the presumption.

## Child Support:

Administrative Rules of Montana. 37.62.101-114. The guidelines are based on the principle that it is the first priority of parents to meet the needs of the child according to the financial ability of the parents. In a dissolution of marriage or when parents have never been married, a child's standard of living should not, to the degree possible, be adversely affected because a child's parents are not living in the same household. The guidelines create a presumption of the adequacy and reasonableness of child support awards. However, every case must be determined on its own merits and circumstances and the presumption may be rebutted by evidence that a child's needs are or are not being met. The support order may vary from the guidelines in a particular case only if the support order contains a specific written finding showing justification that application of the guidelines would be unjust or inappropriate, based upon evidence sufficient to rebut the presumption.

Child support may be determined by agreement of the parties, but may depart from the guidelines only if sufficient justification in writing is presented, and the parties acknowledge the amount that would be required under the guidelines. Income used is actual income from all sources except certain public assistance grants; deductions from income are permitted for court-ordered alimony (maintenance) and child support, health insurances, taxes, social security and certain other allowable expenses. Child support is determined by combining the parents' incomes then applying a standard basic multiplier as listed in the rules and adding certain supplemental amounts (for example, for child care and health insurance), then factoring in a standard of living allowance (to ensure a child's minimum standard of living is maintained). Child support amounts are adjusted for extended time spent with both parents (at least 110 days).

Modification is permitted upon a showing of changed circumstances so substantial and continuing as to make the terms unconscionable or upon written consent of the parties or by a court. Modification is only as to installments due after the actual notice to the parties of a motion for modification.

**Agency:**
Child Support Enforcement Division
Department of Social and Rehabilitation Services
P.O. Box 202943
Helena, MT 59620
406-444-6856
800-346-5437

**Website:**
www.dphhs.mt.gov

# NEBRASKA

**Law:**
Revised Statutes of Nebraska. Neb. Rev. Stat. Sec.

**Paternity:**
Neb. Rev. Stat. Sec. 42-377. Children born to the parties, or to the wife, in a marriage relationship, which may be dissolved or annulled, shall be legitimate.

Neb. Rev. Stat. Sec. 43-1402. A father of a child whose paternity is established, either by judicial proceedings or by acknowledgment, is liable for child support to the same extent as the father of a child born in marriage.

Neb. Rev. Stat. Sec. 43-1409. An acknowledgment includes a statement by the mother consenting to the acknowledgment of paternity and a statement that the man is the biological father of the child and a statement by the father that he is the biological father of the child. A notarized acknowledgment of paternity creates a rebuttable presumption of paternity. The acknowledgment may be withdrawn within the earlier of sixty days or the date of a proceeding relating to the child. After that rescission period a signed, notarized acknowledgment is considered a legal finding which may be challenged only on the basis of fraud, duress, or material mistake of fact. The legal responsibilities, including the child support obligation, of any signatory arising from the acknowledgment shall not be suspended during the challenge, except for good cause shown.

**Child Support:**
Nebraska Child Support Guidelines. The child support guidelines are presumed to be correct. The guidelines consider the combined income of the parents. The court shall consider the earning capacity

of each parent and the guidelines for the establishment of child support obligations. Income less taxes, social security deductions, health insurance, mandatory retirement contributions, and child support is combined (except public assistance benefits and payments received for children of prior marriages). The total amount is then matched to the support table based on the number of children, then the percentage of contribution of each parent is determined. Visitation adjustments or direct cost sharing is permitted as an adjustment to the guidelines. Special worksheets are available for joint physical and split custody situations. If there is evidence of an abusive disregard of the use of child support money paid by one party to the other, the court may require the party receiving such payment to file a verified report with the court, as often as the court requires, stating the manner in which such money is used.

All stipulated agreements for child support must be reviewed against the guidelines and if a deviation exists and is approved by the court, specific findings giving the reason for the deviation must be made. Findings must state the amount of support that would have been required under the guidelines and include a justification of why the order varies from the guidelines. Deviations must take into consideration the best interests of the child. Deviations from the guidelines are permissible when: there are extraordinary medical costs of either parent or child; special needs of a disabled child exist; if total net income exceeds $10,000 monthly; or, the application of the guidelines in an individual case would be unjust or inappropriate.

Modification is permitted for a material change in circumstances such as a variation by at least 10%, but not less than $25 upward or downward, of the current child support obligation as a result of the application of the guidelines. Financial circumstances that have lasted three months and are reasonably expected to last for an additional six months, establish a rebuttable presumption of a material change of circumstances.

**Agency:**
Child Support Enforcement Office
Department of Health and Human Services
P.O. Box 94728
Lincoln, NE 68509
402-471-9160
877-631-9973 (in-state only)

**Website:**
www.hhs.state.ne.us/cse/cseindex.htm

## NEVADA

**Law:**
Nevada Revised Statutes Annotated. Nev. Rev. Stat. Ann. Sec.

**Paternity:**
Nev. Rev. Stat. Ann. Secs. 126.051. A man is presumed to be the natural father of a child if: (a) he and the child's natural mother are or have been married to each other and the child is born during the marriage, or within 285 days after the marriage is terminated by death, annulment, declaration of invalidity or divorce, or after a decree of separation is entered by a court; (b) he and the child's natural mother were cohabiting for at least six (6) months before the period of conception and continued to cohabit through the period of conception; (c) before the child's birth, he and the child's natural mother have attempted to marry each other by a marriage solemnized in apparent compliance with law, although the attempted marriage is invalid or could be declared invalid, and (1) if the attempted marriage could be declared invalid only by a court, the child is born during the attempted marriage, or within 285 days after its termination by death, annulment, declaration of invalidity or divorce, or (2) if the attempted marriage is invalid without a court order, the child is born within 285 days after the termination of cohabitation; (d) while the child is under the age of majority, he receives the child into his home and openly holds out the child as his natural child; or, (e) DNA tests show a 99% probability that he is the father.

Nev. Rev. Stat. Ann. Secs. 126.053. A notarized acknowledgment of paternity creates a finding of paternity if not withdrawn. The acknowledgment may be withdrawn within the earlier of sixty days or the date of a proceeding relating to the child. After that rescission period a signed, notarized acknowledgment is considered a legal finding which may be challenged only on the basis of fraud, duress, or material mistake of fact. Except upon a showing of good cause, a person's obligation for the support of a child must not be suspended during a hearing to challenge a voluntary acknowledgment of paternity.

**Child Support:**
Nev. Rev. Stat. Ann. Secs. 125B.070–125B.080. The guidelines are factored on the gross income of the parent without custody based on the following percentages of income: one child (18%), two children (25%), three children (29%), four children (31%), and for each additional child, an additional 2%. If the parties agree as to the amount of support required, and certify that their agreement is consistent with the appropriate statutory formula or justify why the support deviates from the formula, a court will enter that order. Deviations are permitted for health care, child care, and educational expenses and other extraordinary expenses as listed in the statute.

Amounts not paid become judgments for the sum due. Past due sums must be paid even if the child reaches the age of 18. Handicapped children are entitled to be supported until the handicap is removed or the child becomes self-supporting. A request for modification may be made every three years or at any time on the basis of changed circumstances. A change of 20% or more in the gross monthly income of a person who is subject to an order for the support of a child constitutes changed circumstances.

**Agency:**
Child Support Enforcement Program
Nevada State Welfare Division
1470 East College Parkway
Carson City, NV 89706
775-684-0704
800-992-0900 ext. 4744

**Website:**
www.welfare.state.nv.us/child.htm

# NEW HAMPSHIRE

**Law:**
New Hampshire Statutes Annotated. N.H. Rev. Stat. Ann. Sec.

**Paternity:**
N.H. Rev. Stat. Ann. Sec. 168-B:3. Notwithstanding any other provision of law, a man is presumed to be the father of a child if: (a) he and the child's mother are or have been married to each other and the child is born during the marriage, or within 300 days after the marriage is terminated for any reason, or after a decree of separation is entered by a court; (b) before the child's birth, he and the child's mother have attempted to marry each other by a marriage solemnized in apparent compliance with law, although the attempted marriage is or could be declared void, voidable, or otherwise invalid, and (1) if the attempted marriage could be declared invalid only by a court, the child is born during the attempted marriage, or within 300 days after its termination for any reason, or (2) if the attempted marriage is invalid without a court order, the child is born within 300 days after the termination of cohabitation; (c) after the child's birth, he and the child's mother have married, or attempted to marry each other by a marriage solemnized in apparent compliance with law, although the attempted marriage is or could be declared void, voidable, or otherwise invalid, and (1) he has acknowledged his paternity of the child in a writing filed with the appropriate court or state agency, (2) with his consent, he is named as the child's father on the birth certificate, or (3) he is obligated to support the child under a written voluntary promise or by court order; or, (d) while the child is under the age of majority, he receives the child into his home and openly holds out the child as his child.

N.H. Rev. Stat. Ann. Sec. 5-C:11. Paternity may be established by acknowledgment, called an affidavit of paternity. An affidavit of paternity is considered a legal finding of paternity unless any party withdraws (rescinds) the acknowledgment within the earlier of sixty days or the date of an administrative or judicial proceeding relating to the child, including a proceeding to establish a support order, in which the parent is a party.

**Child Support:**
N.H. Rev. Stat. Ann. Secs. 485-C:1–458-C:7. There is a rebuttable presumption that the amount of the child support award in the guidelines is the correct amount of child support.

Child support is determined by multiplying the parents' combined net income, as defined in the statute, by the appropriate percentage, which is derived from the table and based on the number of children. The formula is one child (25%), two children (33%), three children (40%), and four or more children is 45% of net income. That amount is divided between the parents in proportion to their respective incomes (as adjusted). Adjustments to the guidelines are made under special circumstances (such as for extraordinary medical expenses). Deviation is permitted where application of the guidelines would be unjust or inappropriate in a particular case.

Each child support order shall include the court's determination and findings relative to health insurance and the payment of uninsured medical expenses for the children. All will provide for the assignment of the wages of the responsible parent. All support payments are considered judgments when due and payable and a lien shall be automatic against real and personal property for child support arrearages owed by an obligor who resides or owns property in the state and shall incorporate any unpaid child support which may accrue in the future.

Modification requests are permitted three (3) years after the entry of the last order for support, without the need to show a substantial change of circumstances. No modification of a support order shall apply to any past sums due prior to the date of filing the motion for modification.

**Agency:**
Division of Child Support Services
Health and Human Services Building
129 Pleasant Street
Concord, NH 03301
603-271-4427
800-852-3345 ext. 4427 (in-state only)

**Website:**
www.dhhs.state.nh.us/dhhs/dcss

# NEW JERSEY

**Law:**
New Jersey Statutes Annotated. N.J. Stat. Ann. Sec.

**Paternity:**
N.J. Stat. Ann. Sec. 9:17-43.a. A man is presumed to be the biological father of a child if: (1) he and the child's biological mother are
or have been married to each other and the child is born during the
marriage, or within 300 days after the marriage is terminated by
death, annulment, or divorce; (2) before the child's birth, he and the
child's biological mother have attempted to marry each other by a
marriage solemnized in apparent compliance with law, although the
attempted marriage is or could be declared invalid, and (a) if the
attempted marriage could be declared invalid only by a court, the
child is born during the attempted marriage, or within 300 days
after its termination by death, annulment, or divorce, or (b) if the
attempted marriage is invalid without a court order, the child is
born within 300 days after the termination of cohabitation; (3) after
the child's birth, he and the child's biological mother have married,
or attempted to marry, each other by a marriage solemnized in
apparent compliance with law, although the attempted marriage is
or could be declared invalid, and (a) he has acknowledged his paternity of the child in writing filed with the local registrar of vital statistics, (b) he has sought to have his name placed on the child's birth
certificate as the child's father, pursuant to law, or (c) he openly
holds out the child as his natural child, or (d) he is obligated to support the child under a written voluntary agreement or court order;
(4) while the child is under the age of majority, he receives the child
into his home and openly holds out the child as his natural child;
(5) while the child is under the age of majority, he provides support
for the child and openly holds out the child as his natural child; or
(6) he acknowledges his paternity of the child in a writing filed with
the local registrar of vital statistics, which shall promptly inform the

mother of the filing of the acknowledgment, and she does not dispute the acknowledgment within a reasonable time after being informed thereof, in a writing filed with the local registrar.

N.J. Stat. Ann. Sec. 26:8-28–26:8-30. Paternity may be established by both parents signing an acknowledgment, called a certificate of parentage. The Certificate must be notarized. A signed voluntary acknowledgment of paternity is considered a legal finding of paternity subject to the right of a parent to withdraw (rescind) the acknowledgment within sixty days of the date of signing, or by the date of establishment of a support order to which the parent is a party, whichever is earlier. An adjudication of paternity shall only be voided upon a finding that there exists clear and convincing evidence of fraud, duress, or a material mistake of fact. The legal responsibilities of any signatory arising from the acknowledgment may not be suspended during the challenge, except for good cause shown.

**Child Support:**
New Jersey Rules of Court Appendix IX. The guidelines were developed to provide the court with economic information to assist in the establishment and modification of fair and adequate child support awards. The premise of the guidelines is that (1) child support is a continuous duty of both parents, (2) children are entitled to share in the current income of both parents, and (3) children should not be the economic victims of divorce or out-of-marriage birth. The economic data and procedures of the guidelines attempt to simulate the percentage of parental net income that is spent on children in intact families. The guidelines establish a presumption that the amount calculated to apply to the parties' case is correct. Deviation from the guidelines is permitted where a party proves to the court that circumstances exist that make a guidelines-based award inappropriate in a specific case, such as where the children have special needs or due to the circumstances of the parents.

This state combines each parent's net income, then apportions the percentage of each parent's share based on tables. In sole-parenting situations, the custodial parent's share of the child-rearing expenses is assumed to be spent directly on the child. The noncustodial parent's share of child-rearing costs represents the support order that is paid to the custodial parent for the benefit of the child. In situations involving visitation or shared-parenting, both parents make direct expenditures for the child while the child resides in their homes. Certain expenses such as health, education, and child care expenses and other extraordinary expenses may be added to the basic child support obligation. Adjustments are also made for extended visitation and shared parenting time.

Modification is permitted where the circumstances of the parties have changed since the date that the order was entered.

**Agency:**
Division of Family Development
Department of Human Services
Bureau of Child Support and Paternity Programs
P.O. Box 716
Trenton, NJ 08625
609-588-2915
800-621-5437 (in-state only)
877-655-4371 (automated system)

**Website:**
www.njchildsupport.org

# NEW MEXICO

**Law:**
New Mexico Statutes Annotated. N.M. Stat. Ann. Sec.

**Paternity:**
N.M. Stat. Ann. Sec. 40-11-5. A man is presumed to be the natural father of a child if: (1) he and the child's natural mother are or have been married to each other and the child is born during the marriage or within 300 days after the marriage, is terminated by death, annulment, declaration of invalidity or dissolution of marriage, or after a decree of separation is entered by a court; (2) before the child's birth, he and the child's natural mother have attempted to marry each other by a marriage solemnized in apparent compliance with law, although the attempted marriage is or could be declared invalid, and (a) if the attempted marriage could be declared invalid only by a court, the child is born during the attempted marriage or within 300 days after its termination by death, annulment, declaration of invalidity, or divorce, or (b) if the attempted marriage is invalid without a court order, the child is born within three hundred days after the termination of cohabitation; (3) after the child's birth, he and the child's natural mother have married or attempted to marry each other by a marriage solemnized in apparent compliance with law, although the attempted marriage is or could be declared invalid, and (a) he has acknowledged his paternity of the child in writing filed with the vital statistics bureau of the public health division of the department of health, (b) with his consent, he is named as the child's father on the child's birth certificate, or (c) he is obligated to support the child under a written voluntary promise or by court order; (4) while the child is under the age of majority, he openly holds out the child as his natural child and has established a personal, financial, or custodial relationship with the child; or, (5) he acknowledges his

paternity of the child and the mother upon notice does not dispute the acknowledgment.

A signed voluntary acknowledgment of paternity is considered a legal finding of paternity, subject to the right of any signatory to rescind the acknowledgment within the earlier of sixty days from the date of signing or the date of a proceeding relating to the child to which the signatory is a party. After that period, the acknowledgment may be challenged in court only on the grounds of fraud, duress, or material mistake of fact. Legal responsibilities arising from signing the acknowledgment may not be suspended during the challenge, except upon a showing of good cause.

**Child Support:**
N.M. Stat. Ann Secs. 40-4-11.1–40-4-11.6. The child support guidelines are presumed to correctly establish the child support due. The purposes of the child support guidelines are to: (1) establish as state policy an adequate standard of support for children, subject to the ability of parents to pay; (2) make awards more equitable by ensuring more consistent treatment of persons in similar circumstances; and, (3) improve the efficiency of the court process by promoting settlements and giving courts and the parties guidance in establishing levels of awards.

The guidelines are based on the proportionate share of the combined actual gross income of both parents less public assistance and child support received as applied to the schedule of support for the correct number of children. In shared custody cases, each parent's responsibility for direct expenses is deducted from that parent's basic obligation and the difference, if any, is the support due and owing. In sole custody situations, adjustments may be made for extended visitation.

Deviations from the guidelines are permitted if application would produce unjust or inappropriate results. Every decree or judgment of child support that deviates from the guideline amount shall contain a statement of the reasons for the deviation.

Modification is permitted upon a showing of material and substantial changes in circumstances after the entry of the order. There will be a presumption of substantial change if there is at least a 20% change in the order based upon application of the guidelines where the petition for modification is filed more than one year after the filing of the preexisting order.

**Agency:**
Child Support Enforcement Bureau
Department of Human Services
P.O. Box 25110
Santa Fe, NM 87504

*Street Address:*
2009 South Pacheco
Pollen Plaza
Santa Fe, NM 87504
800-585-7631

**Website:**
www.state.nm.us/hsd/csed.html

# NEW YORK

**Law:**
*McKinney's* Consolidated Laws of New York Annotated, Domestic Relations law. N.Y. Dom. Rel. Law Sec.

**Paternity:**
N.Y. Dom. Rel. Law Sec. 24. A man is presumed to be the father of a child if he marries the mother and the child is born to them before or after the marriage, even if it is later declared invalid. Paternity may also be established by court proceeding or by acknowledgment.

N.Y. Family Court Act Sec. 516a. Paternity may be established by acknowledgment. The acknowledgment must be in writing and filed with the registrar of the district in which the birth occurred and in which the birth certificate has been filed. No further proceedings are necessary to establish paternity. The acknowledgment may be withdrawn (rescinded) by either party's filing of a petition with the court to vacate the acknowledgment within the earlier of sixty days of the date of signing the acknowledgment or the date of an administrative or a judicial proceeding (including a proceeding to establish a support order) relating to the child in which either parent is a party. After that period, either signer of the acknowledgment may challenge the acknowledgment of paternity in court only on the basis of fraud, duress, or material mistake of fact. Upon receiving a party's challenge to an acknowledgment, the court will order DNA tests for the determination of the child's paternity and will make a finding. The legal obligations, including the obligation for child support arising from the acknowledgment, may not be suspended during the challenge to the acknowledgment except for good cause shown to the court.

**Child Support:**
N.Y. Dom. Rel. Law Sec. 240(1-b). The proportionate percentage of combined parental income is determined by the guidelines based on the number of children to be supported. The amount of the basic child support obligation is determined by combining parental income, multiplying the combined parental income up to $80,000 by the appropriate child support percentage, and then prorating that proportion. Child support percentages are: 17% (one child), 25% (two children), 29% (three children), 31% (four children), and no less than 35% for five or more children. To this is added health care, child care, and certain other expenses in prorated amounts.

Deviations may be made if the guideline amounts are unjust or inappropriate. The parties may agree to child support, but any agreement must include a provision stating that the parties have been advised of the guidelines, and that they are presumptively correct. If the agreement deviates from the guideline amounts, the agreement must specify the guideline amount and the reason or reasons that the agreement does not provide for payment of that amount. Any court order or judgment incorporating a validly executed agreement which deviates from the basic child support obligation must set forth the court's reasons for doing so.

Modification is permitted upon substantial change in circumstance since the entry of the order. Where parties have agreed to child support and that is incorporated into a judgment or order, the parent seeking to modify child support provisions must demonstrate either that the agreement was unfair or inequitable when made, that an unanticipated or unreasonable change in circumstances has occurred, or that the custodial parent is unable to meet the needs of or provide adequate support for the child. No modification can reduce any past-due child support which accrued prior to the date of filing the request to modify the child support order.

**Agency:**

Division Child Support Enforcement
Office of Temporary and Disability Assistance
40 North Pearl Street
13th Floor
Albany, NY 12243
518-474-9081
800-208-4485

**Website:**

www.newyorkchildsupport.com

# NORTH CAROLINA

## Law:

North Carolina General Statutes. N.C. Gen. Stat. Sec.

## Paternity:

When a child is born during marriage or if the parties marry after the child is born, the state presumes it is the child of the husband. Paternity may also be established by petition or acknowledgment.

N.C. Gen. Stat. Sec. 110-132. A written acknowledgment, called an affidavit of parentage, signed by the father and mother of the child constitutes an admission of paternity and has the same legal effect as a judgment of paternity for the purpose of establishing child support. Either party may withdraw (rescind) the affidavit within the earlier of sixty days of the date of signing or the date of entry of an order establishing paternity or an order for the payment of child support. To withdraw, a party must petition the court. After that period, an affidavit may be challenged in court only upon the basis of fraud, duress, mistake, or excusable neglect. The legal responsibilities, including child support obligations, of any parent may not be suspended during the challenge except for good cause shown.

## Child Support:

North Carolina Child Support Guidelines. The child support guidelines apply as a rebuttable presumption and must be used when the court enters a child support order. The guidelines are based on the income shares model, which considers a shared parental obligation determined by the combined adjusted gross income applied to a support table listing the number of children. Child care, health insurance, and extraordinary costs may be added to the basic child support amount.

Deviation from the guidelines is permitted where application would be inequitable to one of the parties or to the child.

Modification is permitted upon a showing that there has been a sub-stantial change of circumstances, or for an order which is at least three years old, a deviation of 15% or more between the amount of the existing order and the amount of child support resulting from application of the guidelines will warrant modification.

**Agency:**
Child Support Enforcement Division
Division of Social Services
Department of Human Resources
P.O. Box 20800
Raleigh, NC 27619
919-225-3800
800-992-9457 (in-state only)

**Website:**
www.dhhs.state.nc.us/dss/cse

# NORTH DAKOTA

**Law:**
North Dakota Century Code Annotated. N.D. Cent. Code Sec.

**Paternity:**
N.D. Cent. Code Sec. 14-17-04. A man is presumed to be the biological father of a child if: the man and the child's biological mother are or have been married to each other and the child is born during the marriage or within three hundred days after the marriage is terminated by death, annulment, declaration of invalidity, or divorce, or after a decree of separation is entered by a court; before the child's birth, that man and the child's biological mother have attempted to marry each other by a marriage solemnized in apparent compliance with law, although the attempted marriage is or could be declared invalid, and (1) if the attempted marriage could be declared invalid only by a court, the child is born during the attempted marriage or within three hundred days after its termination by death, annulment, declaration of invalidity, or divorce, or (2) if the attempted marriage is invalid without a court order, the child is born within three hundred days after the termination of cohabitation; after the child's birth, that man and the child's biological mother have married or attempted to marry each other by a marriage solemnized in apparent compliance with law, although the attempted marriage is or could be declared invalid, and (1) the man has acknowledged his paternity of the child in writing filed with the division of vital statistics of the state department of health, (2) with the man's consent, that man is named as the child's father on the child's birth certificate, or (3) the man is obligated to support the child under a written voluntary promise or by court order; while the child is under the age of majority, the man receives the child into his home and openly holds out the child as his biological child; the man acknowledges the man's paternity of the child in a writing filed with the division of vital statistics of the state department of health,

which shall promptly inform the mother of the filing of the acknowledgment, and the mother does not dispute the acknowledgment within a reasonable time after being informed of the acknowledgment, in a writing filed with the division of vital statistics of the state department of health; or, if DNA tests show at least a 95% probability that the man is the father.

N.D. Cent. Code Secs. 14-19-03–14-19-10. The relationship of father and child may be established by an acknowledgment of paternity, which is made on an approved form signed by both parents, given before a witness. An acknowledgment acts as a presumption establishing paternity. An acknowledgment of paternity may be vacated by the court or state department of health or rescinded by the mother or father by a notarized writing signed by either the father or the mother and filed with the state department of health within the earlier of sixty days after the execution of the acknowledgment of paternity or the date of any proceeding relating to the child in which the signatory on the acknowledgment is a party. Within one (1) year a party may also ask a court to vacate an acknowledgment upon a showing, by a party, that an acknowledgment of paternity was the result of material mistake of fact, fraud, or duress. The time may be extended in certain extenuating circumstances, such as where the claim could not be discovered earlier. The legal responsibilities of a parent, including the duty of supporting the child, may not be suspended during a district court proceeding under this section, except for good cause shown.

**Child Support:**
North Dakota Administrative Code Secs. 75-02-04.1 et seq. Child support is determined based on the net income of the noncustodial parent matched to a support schedule for the correct number of children to be supported. Deviations are permitted based on the factors identified in the code.

**Agency:**
Department of Human Services
Child Support Enforcement Agency
P.O. Box 7190
Bismarck, ND 58507
701-328-7509
800-755-8530 (in-state only)

**Website:**
www.nd.gov/humanservices/services/childsupport

## OHIO

**Law:**
*Page's* Ohio Revised Code Annotated. Ohio Rev. Code Ann. Sec.

**Paternity:**
Ohio Rev. Code Ann. Sec. 3111.03. A man is presumed to be the natural father of a child under any of the following circumstances: (1) The man and the child's mother are or have been married to each other, and the child is born during the marriage or is born within three hundred days after the marriage is terminated by death, annulment, divorce, or dissolution or after the man and the child's mother separate pursuant to a separation agreement. (2) The man and the child's mother attempted, before the child's birth, to marry each other by a marriage that was solemnized in apparent compliance with the law of the state in which the marriage took place, the marriage is or could be declared invalid, and either of the following applies: (a) the marriage can only be declared invalid by a court and the child is born during the marriage or within three hundred days after the termination of the marriage by death, annulment, divorce, or dissolution, or (b) the attempted marriage is invalid without a court order and the child is born within three hundred days after the termination of cohabitation.

Ohio Rev. Code Ann. Sec. 3111.23 to 3111.28. An acknowledgment signed and notarized by both parents and filed with the office of child support operates as a legal finding of paternity. Once the acknowledgment becomes final the man who signed the acknowledgment of paternity assumes the parental duty of support. A request to rescind must be made within sixty days. After that period, the party seeking to withdraw the acknowledgment must prove fraud, duress, or material mistake of fact in a court proceeding filed within one year of the acknowledgment becoming final.

**Child Support:**
Ohio Rev. Code Ann. Secs. 3113.215 et seq. The guidelines are based on proportionate percentages of adjusted gross income (excluding public assistance and prior child support received) of both parents. Adjustments permit deductions for taxes, social security, and prior support orders paid (child and spouse). The guideline schedule is then applied to the income amount to determine the basic child support obligation. To that amount is added health insurance expenses and certain child care expenses. Except when the parents have split parental rights and responsibilities, a parent's child support obligation for a child for whom the parent is the residential parent and legal custodian shall be presumed to be spent on that child and shall not become part of a child support order, and a parent's child support obligation for a child for whom the parent is not the residential parent and legal custodian shall become part of a child support order. If the parents have split parental rights and responsibilities, the child support obligations of the parents shall be offset, and the court shall issue a child support order requiring the parent with the larger child support obligation to pay the net amount pursuant to the child support order.

A court may deviate from the guidelines where they would be unjust or inappropriate and not be in the best interest of the child (such as for special needs or extraordinary obligations related to the child or for extended visitation). Modification requests are permitted if the application of the guidelines would result in a 10% change in support or upon proof of a substantial change in circumstances.

**Agency:**
Office of Child Support Enforcement
Department of Human Services
30 East Broad Street
30th Floor
Columbus, OH 43266
614-752-6561
800-686-1556

**Website:**
www.jfs.ohio.gov

# OKLAHOMA

**Law:**
Oklahoma Statutes Annotated. Okla. Stat. Ann. tit. Sec.

**Paternity:**
Okla. Stat. Ann. tit. 10, Sec. 2. A man is presumed to be the natural father of a child if: he and the child's natural mother are or have been married to each other and the child is born during the marriage, or within ten months after the termination of the marriage. A child born before the parents are married is presumed to be the child of the parents when they marry. Or, even if the parties do not marry, where the child is born within ten months of the parents living together, parentage is presumed. The man is presumed to be the father of a child if he treated the child as his own for a period of two years. Also, if the United States Citizenship and Immigration Service determined that he was the father of the child at the time of the child's entry into the United States and he had the opportunity at the time of the child's entry to admit or deny the paternal relationship. Finally, paternity will be presumed where DNA tests show a 95% probability of paternity.

Okla. Stat. Ann. tit. 63, Sec. 1-311.3. An affidavit acknowledging paternity on a form prescribed by the Department of Human Services must include a statement by the mother consenting to the assertion of paternity and stating the name of the father and a statement by the father that he is the natural father of the child.

Okla. Stat. Ann. tit. 10, Sec. 70(B). A statement acknowledging paternity has the same legal effect as an order of paternity entered in a court or administrative proceeding. The statement may be rescinded by the mother or acknowledging father within the earlier of sixty days after the statement is signed by filing a signed rescission of affidavit acknowledging paternity form with the Office of the

State Registrar of Vital Statistics, or the date of an administrative or judicial proceeding relating to the child, including but not limited to a proceeding to establish a support order, in which the signatory is a party. After that time, a signed voluntary acknowledgment of paternity may be challenged in court only on the basis of fraud, duress, or material mistake of fact. Legal responsibilities, including child support, of any signatory arising from the acknowledgment will not be suspended during the challenge, except for good cause shown.

**Child Support:**
Okla. Stat. Ann. tit. 43, Secs.118–120. Child support is computed as a percentage of the combined gross income of both parents. Certain adjustments to gross income are permitted. The adjusted gross income of both parents is added together and the Child Support Guideline Schedule (Sec. 119) is used to compute the support amount. Additions to the support amount for health care expenses and certain child care expenses are also prorated between the parents. The noncustodial parent's share is paid to the custodial parent. There are additional special computations for split custody or extended visitation.

The court may deviate from the guidelines where their application would be unjust, inequitable, unreasonable, or inappropriate under the circumstances, or not in the best interests of the children.

Modifications may be made if the support amount is not in accordance with the child support guidelines or upon other material change in circumstances.

**Agency:**
Child Support Enforcement Division
Department of Human Services
P.O. Box 53552
Oklahoma City, OK 73152

*Street Address:*
2409 N. Kelley Avenue
Annex Building
Oklahoma City, OK 73152
405-522-5871
800-522-2922

**Website:**
www.okdhs.org/childsupport

## OREGON

**Law:**
Oregon Revised Statutes Annotated. Or. Rev. Stat. Sec.

**Paternity:**
Or. Rev. Stat. Sec. 109.070. A child born during marriage is presumed to be the child of the mother's husband, whether or not the marriage of the husband and wife may be void; the child is also presumed to be the man's if he married the mother after the birth of the child. Paternity may also be established by a court or by acknowledgment of paternity.

Or. Stat. Ann. Sec. 109.070(2). A party to a voluntary acknowledgment of paternity may rescind the acknowledgment within the earlier of sixty days after filing the voluntary acknowledgment of paternity or the date of a proceeding relating to the child, including a proceeding to establish a support order, in which the party wishing to rescind the acknowledgment is also a party to the proceeding. After that period, an acknowledgment may be challenged on the basis of fraud, duress, or material mistake of fact. There is a provision which allows a challenge to be filed, subject to certain conditions, within one year after the voluntary acknowledgment has been filed. Legal responsibilities arising from the voluntary acknowledgment of paternity, including child support obligations, may not be suspended during the challenge, except for good cause.

**Child Support:**
Oregon Administrative Regulation 137-50-320–137-50-490. The guidelines are based on the combined adjusted gross income of the parents. Gross income is adjusted by child or spousal support obligations. The percentage contribution of each parent to the combined adjusted gross income is determined by dividing the combined adjusted gross income into each parent's adjusted gross

income. Next, the basic child support obligation is determined by application of the guideline percentage amounts. Added to that are health care and certain child care expenses. Although a monetary obligation is computed for each parent, only the noncustodial parent will be ordered to pay support except in shared custody and split custody cases. Special computations are made for split or shared custody (at least 35% parenting time) or for significant parenting time (at least 20%).

Deviations from the guidelines are permitted upon a finding that the amount is unjust or inappropriate (such as special hardships or extraordinary needs). A modification is permitted upon a showing of a change of circumstances or two years must have passed since the effective date of the last support order.

**Agency:**
Oregon Department of Justice
Division of Child Support Enforcement
494 State Street, SE
Salem, OR 97301
503-986-6090
800-850-0228 (in-state only)

**Website:**
www.dcs.state.or.us

## PENNSYLVANIA

**Law:**
*Purdon's* Pennsylvania Consolidated Statutes Annotated. (Title) Pa. Cons. Stat. Sec.

### Paternity:
23 Pa. Cons. Stat. Sec. 5102. Paternity is determined by any one of the following ways: (1) If the parents of a child born out of wedlock have married each other. (2) If, during the lifetime of the child, it is determined by clear and convincing evidence that the father openly holds out the child to be his and either receives the child into his home or provides support for the child. (3) If there is clear and convincing evidence that the man was the father of the child, which may include a prior court determination of paternity.

23 Pa. Cons. Stat. Sec. 5103(a) provides for an acknowledgment of paternity. The father must sign an acknowledgment of paternity and the form must include the consent of the mother of the child, supported by her witnessed statement. An acknowledgment of paternity constitutes conclusive evidence of paternity without further court action. If the mother does not consent, then the father may file the form with the Department of Public Welfare as a claim of paternity. In the absence of the mother's consent, the filing and indexing of a claim of paternity by the father operates to give the father notice of proceedings relating to the child, but does not confer paternity rights (the father could file a proceeding to establish paternity).

23 Pa. Cons. Stat. Sec. 5103(g). An acknowledgment may be challenged within the earlier of sixty days or the date of an administrative or judicial proceeding relating to the child, including, but not limited to, a domestic relations section conference or a proceeding to establish a support order in which the signatory is a party. After that period, the acknowledgment may only be challenged with

proof of clear and convincing evidence of fraud, mistake, or duress. An order for support will not be suspended during the challenge, except for good cause shown.

**Child Support:**
Pennsylvania Rules of Civil Procedure 1910.16-1–1910.16-5. The support guidelines set forth the amount of support which a spouse or parent should pay on the basis of both parties' net monthly incomes and the number of persons being supported. The support of a spouse or child is a priority obligation so that a party is expected to meet this obligation by adjusting his or her other expenditures. There is a presumption that the amount of the award determined from the guidelines is the correct amount of support to be awarded.

The guidelines are based on a percentage of adjusted net income of the parents. Certain proportional adjustments are made based on permitted additional expenses (such as health care). There are currently five percentages applicable in the guidelines based on number of children and income level. The proportionate percentage of each parent's obligation is then determined, and the noncustodial parent pays his or her share to the custodial parent. There are special guideline calculations for divided or split custody arrangements.

Deviations are permitted taking into consideration the special needs and obligations of the parties and the record must include a finding that an award in the amount determined from the guidelines would be unjust or inappropriate (e.g., for unusual needs or certain medical expenses). Modifications are permitted upon a material and substantial change in the support amount. The existence of additional income, income sources, or assets identified through automated methods may also constitute a material and substantial change in circumstances.

**Agency:**
Bureau of Child Support Enforcement
Department of Public Welfare
P.O. Box 8018
Harrisburg, PA 17105
717-783-5184
800-932-0211

**Website:**
www.dpw.state.pa.us/child/childsupport

# RHODE ISLAND

## Law:
General laws of Rhode Island. R.I. Gen. Laws Sec.

## Paternity:
R.I. Gen. Laws Sec. 15-8-3. A man is presumed to be the natural father of a child if: (1) he and the child's natural mother are or have been married to each other and the child is born during the marriage, or within 300 days after the marriage is terminated by death, annulment, declaration of invalidity, or divorce, or after a decree of separation is entered by a court. (2) Before the child's birth, he and the child's natural mother have attempted to marry each other by a marriage solemnized in apparent compliance with law, although the attempted marriage is or could be declared invalid, and (i) if the attempted marriage could be declared invalid only by a court, the child is born during the attempted marriage, or within 300 days after its termination by death, annulment, declaration of invalidity, or divorce, or (ii) if the attempted marriage is invalid without a court order, the child is born within 300 days after the termination of cohabitation. (3) After the child's birth, he and the child's natural mother have married, or attempted to marry, each other by a marriage solemnized in apparent compliance with law, although the attempted marriage could be declared invalid, and (i) he has acknowledged his paternity of the child in writing filed with the clerk of the family court, (ii) with his consent, he is named as the child's father on the child's birth certificate, or (iii) he is obligated to support the child under a written voluntary promise or by court order. (4) He acknowledges his paternity of the child in a writing filed with the clerk of the family court, who shall promptly inform the mother of the filing of the acknowledgment, and she does not dispute the acknowledgment, within a reasonable time after being informed, in a writing filed with the clerk of the family court. (5) Blood testing results conclusively establish paternity. (6) A sworn

acknowledgment of paternity is signed by both parents on the proper forms and is forwarded to the state registrar of vital records for the purpose of amending the birth certificate.

The sworn acknowledgment of paternity becomes a conclusive presumption if there is no court challenge to this acknowledgment within sixty days of signing. The only defenses which may be raised to the signing of this acknowledgment after the sixty (60) day period are fraud, duress, or mistake of fact.

## Child Support:

R.I. Gen. Laws Sec.15-5-16.2. Child Support Guidelines. The court shall order either or both parents owing a duty of support to a child to pay an amount based upon a formula and guidelines adopted by an administrative order of the family court. Support may be ordered through age 18 (or up to ninety (90) days after graduation or age 19, whichever comes first). For children with a severe physical or mental impairment, support may be ordered until the child turns 21 years old.

Modification is permitted every three (3) years. The three (3) year period is not applicable where the modification is requested based upon a substantial change in circumstances. Child support may be modified retroactively only to the date that the other parent was notified that a petition requesting the modification was filed.

**NOTE:** *Child support in Rhode Island is administered by the Department of Human Services, but the program responsible for enforcement is the Division of Taxation—Child Support Enforcement.*

**Agency:**

Rhode Island Child Support Agency
77 Dorrance Street
Providence, RI 02906
401-222-2857

**Website:**

www.dhs.state.ri.us

## SOUTH CAROLINA

**Law:**
Code of Laws of South Carolina S.C. Code Ann. Sec.

**Paternity:**
A husband is presumed to be the father of the wife's child.

S.C. Code Ann. Sec. 20-1-60. Where parents marry after a child is born, the husband is the presumed father of the child.

S.C. Code Ann. Sec 20-1-90. The invalidity of a marriage will not affect the presumption that the husband is the father of a child.

S.C. Code Ann. Sec 20-7-90. Any able-bodied person capable of earning a living who, without just cause, fails to provide reasonable support to his or her dependent child is guilty of a misdemeanor.

S.C. Code Ann. Sec. 20-7-952. Unless the court orders otherwise, the custody of a child born outside of marriage is solely in the natural mother unless the mother has relinquished her rights to the child. If paternity has been acknowledged or determined by a court or administrative proceeding, the father may petition the court for rights of visitation or custody in a proceeding before the court apart from an action to establish paternity.

S.C. Code Ann. Sec. 20-7-956. Paternity can be established by acknowledgment. A sworn acknowledgment of paternity must be signed by both parents. The acknowledgment must include a written certification by a witness that specifies that prior to signing the acknowledgment, the provisions of the acknowledgment were discussed with the person acknowledging paternity and that, based upon this discussion, it is the witness' opinion that the acknowledgment is being given voluntarily and that it is not being obtained under duress or through coercion. A verified voluntary acknowledgment of paternity creates a conclusive presumption of the putative father's paternity subject to the right of rescission.

S.C. Code Ann. Sec. 20-7-958. Any signatory of an acknowledgment can withdraw (rescind) the acknowledgment within the earlier of sixty (60) days or the date of an administrative or judicial proceeding relating to the child including a proceeding to establish a support order in which the signatory is a party. After that period, a verified voluntary acknowledgment of paternity may be challenged in court only on the basis of fraud, duress, or material mistake of fact. In the event of a challenge, legal responsibilities including child support obligations of any signatory arising from the acknowledgment will not be suspended during the challenge, except for good cause shown.

**Child Support:**
South Carolina Social Service Regulations 114-4710–114-4750. The guidelines are based on the combined adjusted gross income of the parents. The adjustments permit deductions for child support and alimony, and additions for medical expenses and child care. The combined income is factored using the guideline schedule based on income and number of children. The parent's proportionate share of support is then determined and the noncustodial parent pays his or her share of support to the custodial parent, who is presumed to pay his or her share directly. There are special calculations for shared parenting and split custody.

Deviations from the guidelines are permitted where application would be inappropriate (such as by agreement of the parties where in the best interests of the child).

**Agency:**
Department of Social Services
Child Support Enforcement Division
P.O. Box 1469
Columbia, SC 29202
803-898-9210
800-768-5858
800-768-6779 (payments)

**Website:**
www.state.sc.us/dss/csed

# SOUTH DAKOTA

## Law:
South Dakota Codified Laws Annotated. S.D. Codified Laws Sec.

## Paternity:
S.D. Codified Laws Secs. 25-5-3; 25-8-57. The husband and wife are presumed to be the parents of any child born to the wife during the marriage or within ten months after the dissolution of the marriage (even if the marriage is invalid). Paternity may also be established in a proceeding or by acknowledgment.

S.D. Codified Laws Sec. 25-8-49-50. An acknowledgment, called an affidavit of paternity, creates a presumption of paternity. The affidavit must be signed under oath by both parents. A signed and notarized affidavit of paternity creates a presumption of paternity and is admissible as evidence of paternity. The affidavit also allows child support to be entered without requiring any further proceedings to establish paternity.

S.D. Codified Laws Sec. 25-8-59. Any action to contest an acknowledgment must be filed in court on the earlier of sixty days after the creation of the presumption of paternity or the date of any proceedings related to the child, except in cases where there are allegations of fraud, duress, or material mistake of fact. In cases involving allegations of fraud, duress, or material mistake of fact, any action contesting a rebuttable presumption of paternity shall be commenced within three years. The payment of child support, or any other legal responsibilities of the parties, may not be suspended during the pendency of the proceedings, except upon a showing of good cause by the moving party.

## Child Support:

S.D. Codified Laws Secs. 25-7-6.1. The guidelines are factored on the combined net income of both parents. Allowable deductions include: income taxes withheld, FICA taxes withheld, retirement contributions, and payments for child or spouse support. The combined net amount is then applied to the guideline schedules based on number of children and each parent's proportionate share is determined. The share of the custodial parent is presumed to be spent directly for the benefit of the child. The share of the noncustodial parent establishes the amount of the child support order.

Deviations are permitted. Among others, deviations may be based on special needs of the child, substantial sharing of parenting time, or other agreement of the parties.

Modifications are permitted upon proof of a change of circumstances. Any past-due support payments are not subject to modification, except back to the date that notice of the petition of the modification of the support obligation was provided to the paying parent.

## Agency:

Division of Child Support
Department of Social Services
700 Governor's Drive
Pierre, SD 57501
605-773-3641
800-286-9145 (active cases)

## Website:

www.state.sd.us/social/dcs

# TENNESSEE

**Law:**
Tennessee Code Annotated. Tenn. Code Ann. Sec.

**Paternity:**
Tenn. Code Ann. Sec. 36-2-304. A man is rebuttably presumed to be the father of a child if: (1) The man and the child's mother are married or have been married to each other and the child is born during the marriage or within three hundred (300) days after the marriage is terminated by death, annulment, declaration of invalidity, or divorce. (2) Before the child's birth, the man and the mother have attempted to marry each other in compliance with the law, although the attempted marriage is or could be declared illegal, void, and voidable. (3) After the child's birth, the man and the mother have married or attempted to marry each other in compliance with the law although such marriage is or could be declared illegal, void, or voidable; and (a) the man has acknowledged his paternity of the child in a writing filed under the putative father registry established by the department of children services, pursuant to Tenn. Code Ann. Sec. 36-2-318, (b) the man has consented in writing to be named the child's father on the birth certificate, or (c) the man is obligated to support the child under a written voluntary promise or by court order. (4) While the child is under the age of majority, the man receives the child into the man's home and openly holds the child out as the man's natural child. (5) DNA tests show a 95% probability of paternity.

Tenn. Code Ann. Sec. 24-7-113. A voluntary acknowledgment of paternity signed by both parents constitutes a legal finding of paternity. Unless withdrawn, the acknowledgment shall be conclusive of that father's paternity without further order of the court. Withdrawal of an acknowledgment shall be by submission of a sworn statement refuting the named father on a form provided by the state registrar. This form must be filed in the office of vital records of the Department of Health or in any judicial or administrative proceeding relating to the child, at which the signatory is a party within sixty (60) days of the date of completion of the acknowledgment; or by the entry of an order by the administrative or judicial tribunal which directs the rescission of such acknowledgment. After that time, the acknowledgment may only be challenged on the basis of fraud, duress, or material mistake of fact.

**Child Support:**
Official Compilation Rules & Regulations of the State of Tennessee Department of Human Services Sec. 1240-2-4. Tennessee made major changes to its guidelines in 2005. It moved from a percentage of income to an income shares formula in which both parent's incomes are considered, and expenditures for child care and medical insurance are considered.

The amount of child support is determined by calculating an adjusted gross income for each parent; subtracting self-employment tax (if any), pre-existing child support orders, and crediting support for other children that a parent is legally responsible for and actually paying. Each parent's adjusted gross income is combined, and the amount is then applied to a child support schedule according to the number of children to be supported  based on the parent's proportionate income. Added to the basic child support amount is children's health insurance premiums and child care expenses. Special educational expenses may also be considered. Adjustments are made for parenting time of less than fifty-three days or more than 121 days.

The parties may agree on a child support amount; however, in cases where the guidelines are not met the parties must provide a justification for the deviation which takes into consideration the best interest of the child and must state the amount which would have been required under the guidelines.

Modification of all orders that existed prior to January 18, 2005, is permitted if the new guidelines would result in a "significant variance." This means at least a 15% difference in the income of the paying parent; a change in the number of children to be supported; a child becoming disabled; or, an agreed order which is at least 15% different than would exist under the new guidelines or, in the case of a low income parent, at least a 7.5% difference exists under the new guidelines.

**Agency:**
Child Support Services
Department of Human Services
Citizens Plaza Building
12th Floor
400 Deadrick Street
Nashville, TN 37248
615-313-4880
800-838-6911

**Website:**
www.state.tn.us/humanserv/child-support.htm

## TEXAS

**Law:**
*Vernon's* Texas Codes Annotated, Family Code. Tex. Family Code Ann. Sec.

**Paternity:**
Tex. Family Code Ann. Sec. 160.204. A man is presumed to be the father of a child if: (1) he is married to the mother of the child and the child is born during the marriage; (2) he is married to the mother of the child and the child is born before the 301st day after the date the marriage is terminated by death, annulment, declaration of invalidity, or divorce; (3) he married the mother of the child before the birth of the child in apparent compliance with law, even if the attempted marriage is or could be declared invalid, and the child is born during the invalid marriage or before the 301st day after the date the marriage is terminated by death, annulment, declaration of invalidity, or divorce; (4) he married the mother of the child after the birth of the child in apparent compliance with law, regardless of whether the marriage is or could be declared invalid, he voluntarily asserted his paternity of the child, and (a) the assertion is in a record filed with the bureau of vital statistics, (b) he is voluntarily named as the child's father on the child's birth certificate, or (c) he promised in a record to support the child as his own; or, (5) during the first two years of the child's life, he continuously resided in the household in which the child resided and he represented to others that the child was his own.

Tex. Family Code Ann. Sec. 160.301. The mother and father may sign an acknowledgment of paternity. An acknowledgment of paternity or denial of paternity signed by a minor is valid.

Tex. Family Code Ann. Sec. 160.307. A signatory may rescind an acknowledgment of paternity by commencing a proceeding to rescind before the earlier of sixty days after the effective date of the acknowledgment or the date of the first hearing in a proceeding to which the signatory is a party before a court relating to the child, including a proceeding that establishes child support. After that time, a signatory of an acknowledgment of paternity may commence a proceeding to challenge the acknowledgment only on the basis of fraud, duress, or material mistake of fact. The proceeding must be commenced before the fourth anniversary of the date the acknowledgment is filed with the bureau of vital statistics.

**Child Support:**
Tex. Family Code Ann. Secs. 154.121–154.133. The amount of child support under the guidelines is presumed to be reasonable and in the best interest of the child. A court may determine that the application of the guidelines would be unjust or inappropriate under the circumstances. The parties may agree on a child support order which deviates from the guidelines as long as there is a determination that the order is in the best interests of the child.

Either or both parents may be ordered to support a child in the manner until the child is age 18 (or graduates from high school), is emancipated, marries, or dies (a disabled child may be supported for an indefinite period). The guidelines calculate support based on net monthly income of the noncustodial parent. The percentages for the paying parent with a net monthly income of less than $6,000 are: one child (20%), two children (25%), three children (30%), four children (35%), five children (40%), and six or more children (not less than the amount for five children).

Deviations are permitted if application of the guidelines would be unjust or inappropriate under the circumstances (such as based on extensive time of possession and access to a child).

Modification is permitted upon proof that the circumstances of the child or parents have substantially changed since the date of the order. It is presumed that circumstances have changed if it has been three years since the order was entered and the monthly amount of the child support award under the order differs by either 20% or $100 from the amount that would be awarded under the child support guidelines.

**Agency:**
Office of the Attorney General
State Office Child Support Division
P.O. Box 12017
Austin, TX 78711
512-460-6000
800-252-8014

**Website:**
www.oag.state.tx.us/child

# UTAH

**Law:**
Utah Code Annotated. Utah Code Ann. Sec.

**Paternity:**
Utah Code Ann. Secs. 30-1-17.2; 78-45a-1. A child born after marriage is presumed to be the child of his or her parents. The father of a child that is born outside of marriage is liable to the same extent as the father of a child born within marriage for the support of his child. Paternity may be determined in a proceeding or by acknowledgment, called a declaration of paternity.

Utah Code. Ann. Sec. 78-45e. A signed voluntary declaration of paternity signed by the parents on the official form is a legal finding of paternity. The voluntary declaration of paternity may be completed and signed any time after the birth of the child. When a father voluntarily declares paternity, his liability for past child support is limited to a period of four years immediately preceding the date that the voluntary declaration of paternity was filed.

Utah Code. Ann. Sec. 78-45e4. Any person who signed the declaration of paternity has the right to withdraw (rescind) the acknowledgment within the earlier of sixty of signing or the date of an administrative or judicial proceeding relating to the child, including a proceeding to establish a support order, in which the signatory is a party. Within the sixty-day period, a voluntary declaration of paternity may be rescinded by filing a voluntary rescission document with the Office of Vital Records. After that period, a declaration of paternity may be challenged in court only on the grounds of fraud, duress, or material mistake of fact. The legal responsibilities, including child support, of any signatory arising from the declaration may not be suspended during a challenge, except for good cause shown. A child support order based on the voluntary declaration of paternity remains in effect during the pendency of any challenge until a final order of the court rescinding the voluntary declaration. If the declaration is rescinded, the father may not recover any child support he provided for the child before entry of the order of rescission.

**Child Support:**
Utah Code Ann. Secs. 78-45-7. The child support guidelines are presumed correct in establishing child support. Child support is based on adjusted gross income and determined by use of the Child Support Obligation table (Sec. 78-45-7.14), which includes income and number of children levels. Adjusted gross income is gross income less alimony previously ordered and paid and child support previously ordered. The parents' child support obligation is divided between them in proportion to their adjusted gross incomes. There are special calculations for split or joint physical custody cases. Child support also may be reduced by 50% for each child for time periods during which the child is with the noncustodial parent twenty-five of any thirty consecutive days.

Parties may agree if the amount equals or exceeds the guidelines amount. In such cases, parties must submit a completed child support worksheet, financial verification required by Sec. 78-45-7.5 (5), and a written statement indicating whether or not the amount of child support requested is consistent with the guidelines.

Medical expenses and income withholding are required. Deviation from the guidelines is permitted upon consideration of the ages, standard of living, and situation of the parties; the wealth and income of the parties; the needs and earning ability of the parties; and, the responsibilities of the parents for the support of others.

Modification requests are permitted at any time if there has been a substantial change in circumstances (at least 15% difference required), or if at least three years have passed since the last order, when the application of the guidelines would cause a 10% change in the amount.

## Agency:

Bureau of Child Support Services
Department of Human Services
P.O. Box 45033
Salt Lake City, UT 84145
801-536-8500
800-257-9156

## Website:

www.ors.state.ut.us

## VERMONT

**Law:**
Vermont Statutes Annotated. (Title) Vt. Stat. Ann. Sec.

**Paternity:**
15 Vt. Stat. Ann. Sec. 308. A person is presumed to be the natural parent of a child if: (1) the parent fails to submit without good cause to genetic testing as ordered; (2) the parents have voluntarily acknowledged parentage; (3) DNA establishes a 98% probability of parentage; or, (4) the child is born while the husband and wife are legally married to each other.

15 Vt. Stat. Ann. Sec. 307. Where the parents of a child are not married, they may acknowledge parentage by filling out and signing a Voluntary Acknowledgment of Parentage form from the Department of Health and by filing the form with the department of health. An acknowledgment of parentage is a presumptive legal determination of parentage upon filing with the department of health.

15 Vt. Stat. Ann. Sec. 307(f). A person who has signed a Voluntary Acknowledgment of Parentage form may rescind the acknowledgment within sixty days after signing the form or prior to a judicial determination of parentage, whichever occurs first. The rescission must be in writing and filed with the Department of Health. After that time, an acknowledgment may be challenged under Vermont Rule of Civil Procedure 60 for reasons such as mistake, inadvertence, surprise, excusable neglect, newly discovered evidence, fraud, or misrepresentation. During the pendency of such a challenge, the legal responsibilities, including child support obligations, of any signatory arising from the acknowledgment may not be suspended during the challenge, except for good cause shown.

## Child Support:

15 Vt. Stat. Ann. Secs. 653–657. The policy behind the guidelines is that parents have the responsibility to provide child support and that child support orders should reflect the true costs of raising children. The guideline calculation is presumed to be correct.

The guidelines are based on available income, which means gross income, less spousal child support actually paid, the cost of health insurance for the children, FICA, and income taxes withheld. Except in cases of shared or split physical custody, the total child support obligation shall be divided between the parents in proportion to their respective available incomes and the noncustodial parent shall be ordered to pay his or her share to the custodial parent. The custodial parent shall be presumed to spend his or her share directly on the child.

Deviations are permitted if the court finds that application of the guidelines is unfair to the child or to any of the parties (taking into account factors such as resources, needs, education, or travel-related expenses).

Modifications are permitted upon a showing of a real, substantial, and unanticipated change of circumstances. If the child support order has not been modified by the court for at least three years, the court may waive the requirement of a showing of a real, substantial, and unanticipated change of circumstances. Modifications may be made only as to future support installments and installments which came due after the date of notice of the motion to modify to the other party.

**Agency:**
Office of Child Support
103 South Main Street
Waterbury, VT 05671
802-241-2313
800-786-3214

**Website:**
www.ocs.state.vt.us

# VIRGINIA

**Law:**
Annotated Code of Virginia. Va. Code Ann. Sec.

**Paternity:**
Where a child is born during marriage the child is considered to be the child of the parties, even if the marriage is later declared invalid. If the parents marry after the child is born, then the child is also considered to be the parties' child.

Va. Code Ann. Sec. 20-49.1. Paternity may also be established by DNA tests, which show a 98% probability of parenthood; the parties acknowledgment of paternity; or, a legal proceeding to establish paternity.

Va. Code Ann. Sec. 20-49.1. An acknowledgment must be signed by the parents, and unless properly rescinded, has the same legal effect as a paternity judgment. The acknowledgment may be withdrawn (rescinded) by either party within sixty days from the date on which it was signed unless an administrative or judicial order relating to the child in an action to which the party seeking rescission is a party is entered prior to the rescission. After that period, the person challenging the statement establishes in a legal proceeding that the statement resulted from fraud, duress, or a material mistake of fact. During the challenge, the legal responsibilities of any person signing it will not be suspended, except for good cause shown.

**Child Support:**
Va. Code Ann. Secs. 20-108.1–20-108.2. There is a presumption that the guidelines are the correct calculation for a child support award. The court may order that support be paid for any child of the parties. The guidelines are based on combined gross income of the parties (excluding child support and certain other benefits) and

determined according to the number of children on the statutory table (Sec. 20-108.2). Additions for health care coverage and extraordinary medical expenses will be made to the basic support amount, and certain child care expenses may also be added. The total monthly child support obligation is divided proportionately between the parents. The monthly obligation of each parent is computed by multiplying each parent's percentage of the parents' combined gross income by the total child support obligation (monthly). Special calculations are made in split custody or shared custody cases.

The court may require a life insurance policy be maintained for the benefit of the children. Parties may agree to support a child over the age of 18. Support may also be ordered continued for any child up to age 19 who is a full-time high school student, not self-supporting, and living in the home of a party. The court may also order the continuation of support for any child over age 18 who is severely and permanently mentally or physically disabled, unable to live independently and support himself, and resides in the home of a parent.

Deviations from the guidelines are permitted where there is a finding that they would be unjust or inappropriate in a particular case (such as based upon the terms of the custody agreement).

Modification is permitted upon change of circumstances. No support order may be retroactively modified, but may relate back to the period during which there is a petition for modification pending, but only from the date that notice of such petition has been given to the responding party.

**Agency:**

Division of Child Support Enforcement
Department of Social Services
7 North Eight Street
Richmond, VA 23219
804-726-7000
800-468-8894 (in-state only)

**Website:**

www.dss.state.va.us/division/dcse

## WASHINGTON

### Law:
*West's* Revised Code of Washington Annotated. Wash. Rev. Code Ann. Sec.

### Paternity:
Wash. Rev. Code Ann. Sec. 26.26.116. A man is presumed to be the father of a child if: the child is born during the marriage (even if it is invalid) or within 300 days after the marriage is terminated; or, after the birth of the child, he and the mother of the child have married each other and he has acknowledged his paternity. A court may also determine a man's paternity.

Wash. Rev. Code Ann. Secs. 26.26.300; 26.26.305. The parents may sign an acknowledgment of paternity. A valid acknowledgment of paternity filed with the state registrar of vital statistics is equivalent to an adjudication of paternity of a child and confers upon the acknowledged father all the rights and duties of a parent.

Wash. Rev. Code. Ann. Sec. 26.26.330. A party to the acknowledgment may withdraw it within the earlier of sixty days or the date of a proceeding related to the child. After that period, a party has two years to file a challenge, but must prove fraud, duress, or material mistake of fact. Except for good cause shown, during the pendency of a proceeding to rescind or challenge an acknowledgment of paternity, the court may not suspend the legal responsibilities of a signatory arising from an acknowledgment, including the duty to pay child support.

### Child Support:
Wash. Rev. Code Ann. Secs. 26.19.001–26.19-100. The goal of the guidelines is to insure that child support orders are adequate to meet a child's basic needs and to provide additional child support commensurate with the parents' income, resources, and standard of living.

The child support obligation is to be equitably apportioned between the parents. The guidelines are based on combined monthly net income and the ages and number of children for whom support is owed. Gross income is adjusted to exclude child support and other designated benefits received. Taxes, FICA, pension, mandatory union dues, and spousal support paid are items deducted from gross income to reach the net income amount.

Deviations may be made upon a showing, among other things, of extraordinary expenses or if the child spends a significant amount of time with the parent who would otherwise owe support. An agreement of the parties is not by itself adequate reason for any deviations from the standard calculation. Written findings are required for deviations from the guidelines.

Modifications are permitted automatically where a court has required periodic adjustments or modifications of child support. A support order may be subject to modification where there has been a change in circumstance or at least one year has passed since the last order was entered.

**Agency:**
Division of Child Support
Department of Social Health Services
P.O. Box 9162
Olympia, WA 98507

*Street Address:*
712 Pear Street, SE
Olympia, WA 98504
360-664-5113
800-457-6202

**Website:**
www.dshs.wa.gov/dcs

## WEST VIRGINIA

**Law:**
West Virginia Code. W. Va. Code Sec.

**Paternity:**
A husband is presumed to be the father of a child born during the marriage.

W. Va. Code Sec. 42-1-6. The husband is presumed to be the parent of his child if he marries the mother after the birth of the child.

W. Va. Code Sec. 48-24-104. Paternity can also be established in a legal proceeding or by acknowledgment.

W. Va. Code Sec. 48-24-106. The parties may sign an acknowledgment of paternity. A written, notarized acknowledgment legally establishes the man as the father of the child for all purposes including child support.

W. Va. Code Sec. 16-5-12(i)(4). An acknowledgment may be withdrawn (rescinded) by a filing with the clerk of the circuit court of the county in which the child resides a verified complaint stating the name of the child, the name of the other parent, the date of the birth of the child, the date of the signing of the affidavit and a statement that he or she wishes to rescind the acknowledgment of the paternity. If the complaint is filed more than sixty days from the date of execution or the date of an administrative or judicial proceeding relating to the child in which the signatory is a party, the complaint must include specific allegations concerning the elements of fraud, duress, or material mistake of fact.

## Child Support:

W. Va. Code Secs. 48-13-101 through 48-13-803. The guidelines for child support award amounts so as to ensure greater uniformity by those persons who make child support recommendations and enter child support orders and to increase predictability for parents, children, and other persons who are directly affected by child support orders. There is a rebuttable presumption that application of these guidelines results in the correct amount of child support to be awarded.

The guidelines are based on adjusted gross income, which means gross income less the payment of previously ordered child or spousal support. Unreimbursed child health care expenses, work-related child care expenses, and any other extraordinary expenses agreed to by the parents or ordered, less any extraordinary credits agreed to by the parents or ordered, are added to the basic child support obligation to determine the total child support obligation. The child support order is determined by dividing the total child support obligation between the parents in proportion to their income. West Virginia provides separate worksheets to be used in determining child support in basic and extended shared parenting cases.

Deviations from the guidelines are permitted if the guidelines are inappropriate in a specific case to accommodate the needs of the child or the circumstances of the parent or parents (such as special needs, educational expenses, or long-distance visitation costs). The reason for the deviation and the amount of the calculated guidelines award must be stated on the record (preferably in writing on the worksheet or in the order).

Modification requests require a substantial change of circumstances. If application of the guideline would result in a new order that is more than 15% different, then the circumstances are considered to be a substantial change.

**Agency:**
Bureau of Child Support Enforcement
Department of Health & Human Resources
350 Capitol Street
Room 147
Charleston, WV 25301
304-558-3780
800-249-3778

**Website:**
www.wvdhhr.org/bcse

# WISCONSIN

## Law:

*West's* Wisconsin Statutes Annotated. Wis. Stat. Ann. Sec.

## Paternity:

Wis. Stat. Ann. Sec. 891.41. A man is presumed to be the natural father of a child if the child is born during a marriage or is conceived before the marriage is ended; he and the child's mother married after the child was born and they had a relationship when the child was conceived; and, no other man has been determined by a court to be the father.

Wis. Stat. Ann. Sec. 891.405. A man is presumed to be the natural father of a child if he and the mother have acknowledged paternity.

Wis. Stat. Ann. Sec. 767.62. A statement acknowledging paternity that is filed with the state registrar is a conclusive determination, which has the same effect as a judgment of paternity.

Wis. Stat. Ann. Sec. 69.15(3)(m). A statement acknowledging paternity that is filed with the state registrar may be rescinded by either person who signed the statement as a parent of the registrant if the person rescinding the statement files with the state registrar a document prescribed by the state registrar for rescinding a state-ment acknowledging paternity within the earlier of sixty days or before the day on which a court or circuit court commissioner makes an order in an action affecting the family involving the man who signed the statement and the child who is the subject of the statement. A minor has the earlier of the first order relating to the child or sixty days after he or she turns age 18 to file the rescission.

A paternity determination may be voided at any time upon a motion or petition stating facts that show fraud, duress, or a mistake of fact. Except for good cause shown, any orders entered, including child support orders, remain in effect during the pendency of a challenge to paternity proceeding.

## Child Support:

Wisconsin Administrative Code Department of Workforce Development (DWD) 40. The guidelines (called a standard) is based on a percentage of the gross income and assets of either or both parents. The guideline is based on the principle that a child's standard of living should, to the degree possible, not be adversely affected because his or her parents are not living together. It determines the percentage of a parent's income and potential income from assets that parents should contribute toward the support of children if the family does not remain together. The guideline determines the minimum amount each parent is expected to contribute to the support of their children. It expects that the custodial parent shares his or her income directly with their children. It also presumes that the basic needs of the children are being met.

A court may order either or both parents to pay an amount reasonable or necessary for child support. The guidelines are based on a percentage of gross income standard: 17% (one child), 25% (two children), 29% (three children), 31% (four children), and 34% (five or more children). There are separate tables for low-income and high-income cases. The guidelines presume that the parent with whom the child usually lives shares income directly with the child, and that the other parent pays a set percentage of income for the well-being of the child. The support amount may be expressed as a percentage of parental income or as a fixed sum, or as a combination of both in the alternative by requiring payment of the greater or lesser of either a percentage of parental income or a fixed sum. Changes to the guidelines in 2004 cover shared-placement and serial family cases.

Modifications are permitted if there has been an unusual change in circumstances or if thirty-three months have passed where the order is not a percentage order.

**Agency:**
Bureau of Child Support
Division of Workforce Development
P.O. Box 7935
Madison, WI 53707

*Street Address:*
201 East Washington Avenue
Room 200
Madison, WI 53707
608-266-9909

**Website:**
www.dwd.state.wi.us/bcs

# WYOMING

## Law:
Wyoming Statutes Annotated. Wyo. Stat. Ann. Sec.

## Paternity:
Wyo. Stat. Ann. Sec. 14-2-102. A man is presumed to be the father of a child if: he and the mother of the child are married to each other and the child is born during the marriage; he and the mother of the child were married to each other and the child is born within 300 days after the marriage is terminated; before the birth of the child, he and the mother of the child married each other in apparent compliance with law, even if the attempted marriage is or could be declared invalid, and the child is born during the invalid marriage or within 300 days after its termination; or, after the birth of the child, he and the mother of the child married each other in apparent compliance with law, whether or not the marriage is or could be declared invalid, and he voluntarily asserted his paternity.

Wyo. Stat. Ann. Sec. 14-2-601. The parents of a child may sign an acknowledgment of paternity with intent to establish the man's paternity. An acknowledgment of paternity may be signed before the birth of the child and takes effect on the birth of the child or the filing of the document with the state Office of Vital Records, whichever occurs later. An acknowledgment may be signed by a minor. A valid acknowledgment of paternity filed with the state Office of Vital Records is the same as an adjudication of paternity of a child, and confers upon the acknowledged father all of the rights and duties of a parent.

A signatory may rescind an acknowledgment of paternity by commencing a proceeding to rescind before the earlier of sixty days after the effective date of the acknowledgment or the date of the first hearing in a proceeding to which the signatory is a party before a court to adjudicate an issue relating to the child, including a proceeding that establishes support. After the period for rescission has expired, a signatory of an acknowledgment of paternity may commence a proceeding to challenge the acknowledgment only on the basis of fraud, duress, or material mistake of fact, and within two years after the acknowledgment or denial is filed with the state Office of Vital Records. Except for good cause shown, during the pendency of a proceeding to rescind or challenge an acknowledgment of paternity, the court may not suspend the legal responsibilities of a signatory arising from the acknowledgment, including the duty to pay child support.

**Child Support:**

Wyo. Stat. Ann. Sec. 20-2-301 (et seq.) The guidelines are based on net income for both parents, which is gross income less personal income taxes, social security deductions, cost of dependent health care coverage for dependent children, actual payments being made under preexisting support orders for current support of other children, other court-ordered support obligations currently being paid, and mandatory pension deductions. The total income is then compared to the guidelines by number of children to be supported. There are special calculations for shared custody cases, and in sole custody cases, where the noncustodial parent has custody of the child for more than fourteen consecutive days, support shall be reduced by 50%.

Parties may agree to child support. All agreements must be accompanied by a financial affidavit on a form approved by the Wyoming Supreme Court (available at the agency listed), which fully discloses the financial status of the parties. The court will compare the guidelines to review the adequacy of child support agreements negotiated by the parties. If the agreed amount departs from the guidelines, the parties must justify the departure on the forms filed with the court.

Deviations are permitted if application of the guidelines would be unjust or inappropriate in that particular case (such as age of child or health, or child care, or education expenses).

In any case in which child support has been ordered to be paid to the clerk of the court, any payment becomes a judgment on the date it is due. A parent owed support may recover from the owing parent reasonable attorney's fees and other costs of enforcing any judgment for child support.

Modification requests are permitted upon a substantial change of circumstances, at any time. Alternatively, a party may seek modification no earlier than six months after the order was entered if the application of the guidelines would result in a 20% change in the amount. An order for child support is not subject to retroactive modification except upon agreement of the parties, or after the date a party receives notice that a petition for modification has been filed.

**Agency:**
Division of Child Support Enforcement
Department of Family Services
2300 Capital Avenue
Hathaway Building
Room 374
Cheyenne, WY 82002
307-777-6948

**Website:**
http://dfsweb.state.wy.us/csehome/cs.htm

# Index

# About the Author

**Mary L. Boland** received her law degree from John Marshall Law School. A longtime victim's advocate, she has worked to pass legislation protecting victims' rights and has served as a consultant on various federal projects. She has been the chair of the Victim's Committee of the Criminal Justice Section of the American Bar Association and co-chair of the Victims Issues Committee of the Prosecutor's Bar Association of Illinois. She is currently a member of the Criminal Justice Council of the ABA.

Ms. Boland is a full-time prosecutor and has served as an adjunct faculty member of Roosevelt University, Governor's State University, and Loyola Law School in Chicago, Illinois.

# Sphinx® Publishing's National Titles
## Valid in All 50 States

## LEGAL SURVIVAL IN BUSINESS

| | |
|---|---|
| ...e Complete Book of Corporate Forms (2E) | $29.95 |
| ...e Complete Hiring and Firing Handbook | $19.95 |
| ...e Complete Limited Liability Company Kit | $24.95 |
| ...e Complete Partnership Book | $24.95 |
| ...e Complete Patent Book | $26.95 |
| ...e Complete Patent Kit | $39.95 |
| ...e Entrepreneur's Internet Handbook | $21.95 |
| ...e Entrepreneur's Legal Guide | $26.95 |
| ...ancing Your Small Business | $16.95 |
| ...ed, Laid-Off or Forced Out | $14.95 |
| ...rm Your Own Corporation (5E) | $29.95 |
| ...e Home-Based Business Kit | $14.95 |
| ...ow to Buy a Franchise | $19.95 |
| ...ow to Form a Nonprofit Corporation (3E) | $24.95 |
| ...ow to Register Your Own Copyright (5E) | $24.95 |
| ...R for Small Business | $14.95 |
| ...corporate in Delaware from Any State | $26.95 |
| ...corporate in Nevada from Any State | $24.95 |
| ...e Law (In Plain English)® for Restaurants | $16.95 |
| ...e Law (In Plain English)® for Small Business | $19.95 |
| ...e Law (In Plain English)® for Writers | $14.95 |
| ...aking Music Your Business | $18.95 |
| ...inding Her Own Business (4E) | $14.95 |
| ...ost Valuable Business Legal Forms You'll Ever Need (3E) | $21.95 |
| ...ofit from Intellectual Property | $28.95 |
| ...otect Your Patent | $24.95 |
| ...e Small Business Owner's Guide to Bankruptcy | $21.95 |
| ...art Your Own Law Practice | $16.95 |
| ...x Power for the Self-Employed | $17.95 |
| ...x Smarts for Small Business | $21.95 |
| ...ur Rights at Work | $14.95 |

## LEGAL SURVIVAL IN COURT

| | |
|---|---|
| ...torney Responsibilities & Client Rights | $19.95 |
| ...ime Victim's Guide to Justice (2E) | $21.95 |
| ...gal Research Made Easy (4E) | $24.95 |
| ...inning Your Personal Injury Claim (3E) | $24.95 |

## LEGAL SURVIVAL IN REAL ESTATE

| | |
|---|---|
| The Complete Kit to Selling Your Own Home5 | $18.95 |
| The Complete Book of Real Estate Contracts | $18.95 |
| Essential Guide to Real Estate Leases | $18.95 |
| Homeowner's Rights | $19.95 |
| How to Make Money on Foreclosures | $16.95 |
| How to Buy a Condominium or Townhome (2E) | $19.95 |
| How to Buy a Condominium or Townhouse | $14.95 |
| How to Buy Your First Home (2E) | $14.95 |
| The Mortgage Answer Book | $14.95 |
| Sell Your Home Without a Broker | $14.95 |
| The Weekend Landlord | $16.95 |
| The Weekend Real Estate Investor | $14.95 |
| Working with Your Homeowners Association | $19.95 |

## LEGAL SURVIVAL IN SPANISH

| | |
|---|---|
| Cómo Comprar su Primera Casa | $8.95 |
| Cómo Conseguir Trabajo en los Estados Unidos | $8.95 |
| Cómo Hacer su Propio Testamento | $16.95 |
| Cómo Iniciar su Propio Negocio | $8.95 |
| Cómo Negociar su Crédito | $8.95 |
| Cómo Organizar un Presupuesto | $8.95 |
| Cómo Solicitar su Propio Divorcio | $24.95 |
| Guía de Inmigración a Estados Unidos (4E) | $24.95 |
| Guía de Justicia para Víctimas del Crimen | $21.95 |
| Guía Esencial para los Contratos de Arrendamiento de Bienes Raices | $22.95 |
| Inmigración y Ciudadanía en los EE.UU. Preguntas y Respuestas | $16.95 |
| Inmigración a los EE.UU. Paso a Paso (2E) | $24.95 |
| Manual de Beneficios del Seguro Social | $18.95 |
| El Seguro Social Preguntas y Respuestas | $16.95 |
| ¡Visas! ¡Visas! ¡Visas! | $9.95 |

## LEGAL SURVIVAL IN PERSONAL AFFAIRS

| | |
|---|---|
| 101 Complaint Letters That Get Results | $18.95 |
| The 529 College Savings Plan (2E) | $18.95 |
| The 529 College Savings Plan Made Simple | $7.95 |
| The Alternative Minimum Tax | $14.95 |
| The Antique and Art Collector's Legal Guide | $24.95 |
| The Childcare Answer Book | $12.95 |
| Child Support | $18.95 |
| The Complete Book of Insurance | $18.95 |
| The Complete Book of Personal Legal Forms | $24.95 |
| The Complete Credit Repair Kit | $18.95 |
| The Complete Legal Guide to Senior Care | $21.95 |
| The Complete Personal Bankruptcy Guide | $21.95 |
| Credit Smart | $18.95 |
| The Easy Will and Living Will Kit | $16.95 |
| Fathers' Rights | $19.95 |
| The Frequent Traveler's Guide | $14.95 |
| File Your Own Divorce (6E) | $24.95 |
| Gay & Lesbian Rights (2E) | $21.95 |
| Grandparents' Rights (4E) | $24.95 |
| How to Parent with Your Ex | $12.95 |
| How to Write Your Own Living Will (4E) | $18.95 |
| How to Write Your Own Premarital Agreement (3E) | $24.95 |
| The Infertility Answer Book | $16.95 |
| Law 101 | $16.95 |
| Law School 101 | $16.95 |
| The Living Trust Kit | $21.95 |
| Living Trusts and Other Ways to Avoid Probate (3E) | $24.95 |
| Make Your Own Simple Will (4E) | $26.95 |
| Mastering the MBE | $16.95 |
| Money and Divorce | $14.95 |
| My Wishes | $21.95 |
| Nursing Homes and Assisted Living Facilities | $19.95 |
| Power of Attorney Handbook (6E) | $24.95 |
| Quick Cash | $14.95 |
| Seniors' Rights | $19.95 |
| Sexual Harassment in the Workplace | $18.95 |
| Sexual Harassment: Your Guide to Legal Action | $18.95 |
| Sisters-in-Law | $16.95 |

| | |
|---|---|
| The Social Security Benefits Handbook (4E) | $1 |
| Social Security Q&A | $1 |
| Starting Out or Starting Over | $1 |
| Teen Rights (and Responsibilities) (2E) | $1 |
| Unmarried Parents' Rights (and Responsibilities)(3E) | $1 |
| U.S. Immigration and Citizenship Q&A (2E) | $1 |
| U.S. Immigration Step by Step (2E) | $2 |
| U.S.A. Immigration Guide (5E) | $2 |
| What They Don't Teach You in College | $1 |
| What to Do—Before "I DO" | $1 |
| When Happily Ever After Ends | $1 |
| The Wills and Trusts Kit (2E) | $2 |
| Win Your Unemployment Compensation Claim (2E) | $2 |
| Your Right to Child Custody, Visitation, & Support | $2 |

# SPHINX® PUBLISHING'S STATE TITLES

**California Titles**

| | |
|---|---|
| How to File for Divorce in CA (5E) | $26.95 |
| How to Settle & Probate an Estate in CA (2E) | $28.95 |
| How to Start a Business in CA (2E) | $21.95 |
| How to Win in Small Claims Court in CA (2E) | $18.95 |
| Landlords' Legal Guide in CA (2E) | $24.95 |
| Make Your Own CA Will | $18.95 |
| Tenants' Rights in CA (2E) | $24.95 |

**Florida Titles**

| | |
|---|---|
| Child Custody, Visitation and Support in FL | $26.95 |
| How to File for Divorce in FL (8E) | $28.95 |
| Incorporate in FL (7E) | $29.95 |
| How to Form a Limited Liability Co. in FL (3E) | $24.95 |
| How to Form a Partnership in FL | $22.95 |
| How to Make a FL Will (7E) | $16.95 |
| How to Win in Small Claims Court in FL (7E) | $18.95 |
| Land Trusts in Florida (7E) | $29.95 |
| Landlords' Rights and Duties in FL (10E) | $24.95 |
| Probate and Settle an Estate in FL (6E) | $29.95 |
| Start a Business in FL (8E) | $29.95 |

**Georgia Titles**

| | |
|---|---|
| How to File for Divorce in GA (6E) | $21.95 |
| How to Start a Business in GA (4E) | $21.95 |

**Illinois Titles**

| | |
|---|---|
| Child Custody, Visitation and Support in IL | $24.95 |
| File for Divorce in IL (4E) | $26.95 |
| How to Make an IL Will (3E) | $16.95 |
| How to Start a Business in IL (4E) | $21.95 |
| Landlords' Legal Guide in IL | $24.95 |

**Maryland, Virginia and the District of Columbia Titles**

| | |
|---|---|
| File for Divorce in MD, VA, and DC (2E) | $29.95 |
| How to Start a Business in MD, VA, or DC | $21.95 |

**Massachusetts Titles**

| | |
|---|---|
| How to Form a Corporation in MA | $24.95 |
| How to Start a Business in MA (4E) | $21.95 |
| Landlords' Legal Guide in MA (2E) | $24.95 |

**Michigan Titles**

| | |
|---|---|
| How to File for Divorce in MI (4E) | $24.95 |
| How to Make a MI Will (3E) | $16.95 |
| How to Start a Business in MI (4E) | $24.95 |

## Minnesota Titles
How to File for Divorce in MN     $21.95
How to Form a Corporation in MN     $24.95
How to Make a MN Will (2E)     $16.95
## New Jersey Titles
File for Divorce in NJ     $24.95
How to Start a Business in NJ     $21.95
## New York Titles
Child Custody, Visitation and Support in NY     $26.95
File for Divorce in NY     $26.95
How to Form a Corporation in NY (2E)     $24.95
How to Make a NY Will (3E)     $16.95
How to Start a Business in NY (3E)     $21.95
How to Win in Small Claims Court in NY (2E)     $18.95
Tenants' Rights in NY     $21.95
## North Carolina and South Carolina Titles
How to File for Divorce in NC (4E)     $26.95
How to Make a NC Will (3E)     $16.95
How to Start a Business in NC or SC     $24.95
Landlords' Rights & Duties in NC     $21.95
## Ohio Titles
How to File for Divorce in OH (3E)     $24.95
How to Form a Corporation in OH     $24.95
How to Make an OH Will     $16.95
## Pennsylvania Titles
Child Custody, Visitation and Support in PA     $26.95
How to File for Divorce in PA (4E)     $26.95
How to Form a Corporation in PA     $24.95
How to Make a PA Will (2E)     $16.95
How to Start a Business in PA (3E)     $21.95
Landlords' Legal Guide in PA     $24.95
## Texas Titles
Child Custody, Visitation and Support in TX     $22.95
File for Divorce in TX (5E)     $27.95
How to Form a Corporation in TX (3E)     $24.95
How to Probate and Settle an Estate in TX (4E)     $26.95
How to Start a Business in TX (4E)     $21.95
How to Win in Small Claims Court in TX (2E)     $16.95
Landlords' Legal Guide in TX     $24.95
Write Your Own TX Will (4E)     $16.95
## Washington Titles
File for Divorce in WA     $24.95

# SPHINX® PUBLISHING ORDER FORM

**SHIP TO:**

| | Terms | F.O.B. | Chicago, IL | Ship Date |
|---|---|---|---|---|

**Charge my:** ☐ VISA ☐ MasterCard ☐ American Express ☐ **Money Order or Personal Check**

Credit Card Number

Expiration Date

| ISBN | Title | Retail |
|---|---|---|
| | **SPHINX PUBLISHING NATIONAL TITLES** | |
| 1-57248-563-9 | 101+ Complaint Letters That Get Results (2E) | $19.95 |
| 1-57248-361-X | The 529 College Savings Plan (2E) | $18.95 |
| 1-57248-483-7 | The 529 College Savings Plan Made Simple | $7.95 |
| 1-57248-460-8 | The Alternative Minimum Tax | $14.95 |
| 1-57248-349-0 | The Antique and Art Collector's Legal Guide | $24.95 |
| 1-57248-347-4 | Attorney Responsibilities & Client Rights | $19.95 |
| 1-57248-482-9 | The Childcare Answer Book | $12.95 |
| 1-57248-382-2 | Child Support | $18.95 |
| 1-57248-487-X | Cómo Comprar su Primera Casa | $8.95 |
| 1-57248-488-8 | Cómo Conseguir Trabajo en los Estado Unidos | $8.95 |
| 1-57248-148-X | Cómo Hacer su Propio Testamento | $16.95 |
| 1-57248-532-9 | Cómo Iniciar su Propio Negocio | $8.95 |
| 1-57248-462-4 | Cómo Negociar su Crédito | $8.95 |
| 1-57248-463-2 | Cómo Organizar un Presupuesto | $8.95 |
| 1-57248-147-1 | Cómo Solicitar su Propio Divorcio | $24.95 |
| 1-57248-507-8 | The Complete Book of Corporate Forms (2E) | $29.95 |
| 1-57248-383-0 | The Complete Book of Insurance | $18.95 |
| 1-57248-499-3 | The Complete Book of Personal Legal Forms | $24.95 |
| 1-57248-528-0 | The Complete Book of Real Estate Contracts | $18.95 |
| 1-57248-500-0 | The Complete Credit Repair Kit | $19.95 |
| 1-57248-458-6 | The Complete Hiring and Firing Handbook | $19.95 |
| 1-57248-484-5 | The Complete Home-Based Business Kit | $14.95 |
| 1-57248-353-9 | The Complete Kit to Selling Your Own Home | $18.95 |
| 1-57248-229-X | The Complete Legal Guide to Senior Care | $21.95 |
| 1-57248-498-5 | The Complete Limited Liability Company Kit | $24.95 |
| 1-57248-391-1 | The Complete Partnership Book | $24.95 |
| 1-57248-201-X | The Complete Patent Book | $26.95 |
| 1-57248-514-0 | The Complete Patent Kit | $39.95 |
| 1-57248-545-0 | The Complete Personal Bankruptcy Guide | $21.95 |
| 1-57248-369-5 | Credit Smart | $18.95 |
| 1-57248-163-3 | Crime Victim's Guide to Justice (2E) | $21.95 |
| 1-57248-251-6 | The Entrepreneur's Internet Handbook | $21.95 |
| 1-57248-235-4 | The Entrepreneur's Legal Guide | $26.95 |
| 1-57248-160-9 | Essential Guide to Real Estate Leases | $18.95 |
| 1-57248-375-X | Fathers' Rights | $19.95 |
| 1-57248-517-5 | File Your Own Divorce (6E) | $24.95 |
| 1-57248-553-1 | Financing Your Small Business | $16.95 |
| 1-57248-459-4 | Fired, Laid-Off or Forced Out | $14.95 |
| 1-57248-516-7 | Form Your Own Corporation (5E) | $29.95 |
| 1-57248-502-7 | The Frequent Traveler's Guide | $14.95 |
| 1-57248-550-7 | Gay & Lesbian Rights (2E) | $21.95 |
| 1-57248-526-4 | Grandparents' Rights (4E) | $24.95 |
| 1-57248-475-6 | Guía de Inmigración a Estados Unidos (4E) | $24.95 |
| 1-57248-187-0 | Guía de Justicia para Víctimas del Crimen | $21.95 |
| 1-57248-253-2 | Guía Esencial para los Contratos de Arrendamiento de Bienes Raíces | $22.95 |

| Qty | ISBN | Title | Retail |
|---|---|---|---|
| ____ | 1-57248-334-2 | Homeowner's Rights | $19.95 |
| ____ | 1-57248-164-1 | How to Buy a Condominium or Townhome (2E) | $19.95 |
| ____ | 1-57248-556-6 | How to Buy a Condominium or Townhouse | $14.95 |
| ____ | 1-57248-384-9 | How to Buy a Franchise | $19.95 |
| ____ | 1-57248-497-7 | How to Buy Your First Home (2E) | $14.95 |
| ____ | 1-57248-390-3 | How to Form a Nonprofit Corporation (3E) | $24.95 |
| ____ | 1-57248-520-5 | How to Make Money on Foreclosures | $16.95 |
| ____ | 1-57248-479-9 | How to Parent with Your Ex | $12.95 |
| ____ | 1-57248-379-2 | How to Register Your Own Copyright (5E) | $24.95 |
| ____ | 1-57248-394-6 | How to Write Your Own Living Will (4E) | $18.95 |
| ____ | 1-57248-156-0 | How to Write Your Own Premarital Agreement (3E) | $24.95 |
| ____ | 1-57248-504-3 | HR for Small Business | $14.95 |
| ____ | 1-57248-230-3 | Incorporate in Delaware from Any State | $26.95 |
| ____ | 1-57248-158-7 | Incorporate in Nevada from Any State | $24.95 |
| ____ | 1-572485-31-0 | The Infertility Answer Book | $16.95 |
| ____ | 1-57248-474-8 | Inmigración a los EE.UU. Paso a Paso (2E) | $24.95 |
| ____ | 1-57248-400-4 | Inmigración y Ciudadanía en los EE. UU. Preguntas y Respuestas | $16.95 |
| ____ | 1-57248-523-X | The Law (In Plain English)® for Restaurants | $16.95 |
| ____ | 1-57248-377-6 | The Law (In Plain English)® for Small Business | $19.95 |
| ____ | 1-57248-476-4 | The Law (In Plain English)® for Writers | $14.95 |
| ____ | 1-57248-453-5 | Law 101 | $16.95 |
| ____ | 1-57248-374-1 | Law School 101 | $16.95 |
| ____ | 1-57248-509-4 | Legal Research Made Easy (4E) | $24.95 |
| ____ | 1-57248-449-7 | The Living Trust Kit | $21.95 |
| ____ | 1-57248-165-X | Living Trusts and Other Ways to Avoid Probate (3E) | $24.95 |
| ____ | 1-57248-511-6 | Make Your Own Simple Will (4E) | $26.95 |
| ____ | 1-57248-486-1 | Making Music Your Business | $18.95 |
| ____ | 1-57248-186-2 | Manual de Beneficios para el Seguro Social | $18.95 |
| ____ | 1-57248-220-6 | Mastering the MBE | $16.95 |
| ____ | 1-57248-455-1 | Minding Her Own Business, 4E | $14.95 |
| ____ | 1-57248-524-8 | Money and Divorce | $14.95 |
| ____ | 1-57248-480-2 | The Mortgage Answer Book | $14.95 |
| ____ | 1-57248-167-6 | Most Val. Business Legal Forms You'll Ever Need (3E) | $21.95 |
| ____ | 1-57248-519-1 | My Wishes | $21.95 |
| ____ | 1-57248-535-3 | Power of Attorney Handbook (6E) | $24.95 |
| ____ | 1-57248-332-6 | Profit from Intellectual Property | $28.95 |
| ____ | 1-57248-329-6 | Protect Your Patent | $24.95 |
| ____ | 1-57248-376-8 | Nursing Homes and Assisted Living Facilities | $19.95 |
| ____ | 1-57248-385-7 | Quick Cash | $14.95 |
| ____ | 1-57248-350-4 | El Seguro Social Preguntas y Respuestas | $16.95 |
| ____ | 1-57248-386-5 | Seniors' Rights | $19.95 |
| ____ | 1-57248-527-2 | Sexual Harassment in the Workplace | $18.95 |

**Form Continued on Following Page**          SubTotal_____

| Qty | ISBN | Title | Retail |
|---|---|---|---|
| | 1-57248-217-6 | Sexual Harassment: Your Guide to Legal Action | $18.95 |
| | 1-57248-378-4 | Sisters-in-Law | $16.95 |
| | 1-57248-219-2 | The Small Business Owner's Guide to Bankruptcy | $21.95 |
| | 1-57248-529-9 | Sell Your Home Without a Broker | $14.95 |
| | 1-57248-395-4 | The Social Security Benefits Handbook (4E) | $18.95 |
| | 1-57248-216-8 | Social Security Q&A | $12.95 |
| | 1-57248-521-3 | Start Your Own Law Practice | $16.95 |
| | 1-57248-328-8 | Starting Out or Starting Over | $14.95 |
| | 1-57248-525-6 | Teen Rights (and Responsibilities) (2E) | $14.95 |
| | 1-57248-457-8 | Tax Power for the Self-Employed | $17.95 |
| | 1-57248-366-0 | Tax Smarts for Small Business | $21.95 |
| | 1-57248-530-2 | Unmarried Parents' Rights (3E) | $16.95 |
| | 1-57248-549-3 | U.S. Immigration and Citizenship Q&A (2E) | $18.95 |
| | 1-57248-387-3 | U.S. Immigration Step by Step (2E) | $24.95 |
| | 1-57248-392-X | U.S.A. Immigration Guide (5E) | $26.95 |
| | 1-57248-478-0 | ¡Visas! ¡Visas! ¡Visas! | $9.95 |
| | 1-57248-477-2 | The Weekend Landlord | $16.95 |
| | 1-57248-557-4 | The Weekend Real Estate Investor | $14.95 |
| | 1-57248-554-X | What They Don't Teach You in College | $12.95 |
| | 1-57248-451-9 | What to Do — Before "I DO" | $14.95 |
| | 1/57248-548-5 | When Happily Ever After Ends | $14.95 |
| | 1-57248-518-3 | The Wills and Trusts Kit (2E) | $29.95 |
| | 1-57248-473-X | Winning Your Personal Injury Claim (3E) | $24.95 |
| | 1-57248-225-7 | Win Your Unemployment Compensation Claim (2E) | $21.95 |
| | 1-57248-333-4 | Working with Your Homeowners Association | $19.95 |
| | 1-57248-380-6 | Your Right to Child Custody, Visitation and Support (3E) | $24.95 |
| | 1-57248-505-1 | Your Rights at Work | $14.95 |

### CALIFORNIA TITLES

| Qty | ISBN | Title | Retail |
|---|---|---|---|
| | 1-57248-489-6 | How to File for Divorce in CA (5E) | $26.95 |
| | 1-57248-464-0 | How to Settle and Probate an Estate in CA (2E) | $28.95 |
| | 1-57248-336-9 | How to Start a Business in CA (2E) | $21.95 |
| | 1-57248-194-3 | How to Win in Small Claims Court in CA (2E) | $18.95 |
| | 1-57248-246-X | Make Your Own CA Will | $18.95 |
| | 1-57248-397-0 | Landlords' Legal Guide in CA (2E) | $24.95 |
| | 1-57248-515-9 | Tenants' Rights in CA (2E) | $24.95 |

### FLORIDA TITLES

| Qty | ISBN | Title | Retail |
|---|---|---|---|
| | 1-57248-396-2 | How to File for Divorce in FL (8E) | $28.95 |
| | 1-57248-490-X | How to Form a Limited Liability Co. in FL (3E) | $24.95 |
| | 1-57071-401-0 | How to Form a Partnership in FL | $22.95 |
| | 1-57248-456-X | How to Make a FL Will (7E) | $16.95 |
| | 1-57248-204-4 | How to Win in Small Claims Court in FL (7E) | $18.95 |
| | 1-57248-540-X | Incorporate in FL (7E) | $29.95 |
| | 1-57248-381-4 | Land Trusts in Florida (7E) | $29.95 |
| | 1-57248-491-8 | Landlords' Rights and Duties in FL (10E) | $24.95 |
| | 1-57248-558-2 | Probate and Settle an Estate in FL (6E) | $29.95 |
| | 1-57248-538-8 | Start a Business in FL (7E) | $29.95 |

### GEORGIA TITLES

| Qty | ISBN | Title | Retail |
|---|---|---|---|
| | 1-57248-340-7 | How to File for Divorce in GA (5E) | $21.95 |
| | 1-57248-493-4 | How to Start a Business in GA (4E) | $21.95 |

### ILLINOIS TITLES

| Qty | ISBN | Title | Retail |
|---|---|---|---|
| | 1-57248-244-3 | Child Custody, Visitation, and Support in IL | $24.95 |
| | 1-57248-510-8 | File for Divorce in IL (4E) | $26.95 |
| | 1-57248-170-6 | How to Make an IL Will (3E) | $16.95 |
| | 1-57248-265-9 | How to Start a Business in IL (4E) | $21.95 |
| | 1-57248-252-4 | Landlord's Legal Guide in IL | $24.95 |

### MARYLAND, VIRGINIA AND THE DISTRICT OF COLUMBIA

| Qty | ISBN | Title | R |
|---|---|---|---|
| | 1-57248-536-1 | File for Divorce in MD, VA, and DC (2E) | $2 |
| | 1-57248-539-6 | Start a Business in MD, VA, or DC (2E) | $2 |

### MASSACHUSETTS TITLES

| Qty | ISBN | Title | R |
|---|---|---|---|
| | 1-57248-115-3 | How to Form a Corporation in MA | $2 |
| | 1-57248-466-7 | How to Start a Business in MA (4E) | $2 |
| | 1-57248-398-9 | Landlords' Legal Guide in MA (2E) | $2 |

### MICHIGAN TITLES

| Qty | ISBN | Title | R |
|---|---|---|---|
| | 1-57248-467-5 | How to File for Divorce in MI (4E) | $2 |
| | 1-57248-182-X | How to Make a MI Will (3E) | $1 |
| | 1-57248-468-3 | How to Start a Business in MI (4E) | $2 |

### MINNESOTA TITLES

| Qty | ISBN | Title | R |
|---|---|---|---|
| | 1-57248-142-0 | How to File for Divorce in MN | $2 |
| | 1-57248-179-X | How to Form a Corporation in MN | $2 |
| | 1-57248-178-1 | How to Make a MN Will (2E) | $1 |

### NEW JERSEY TITLES

| Qty | ISBN | Title | R |
|---|---|---|---|
| | 1-57248-512-4 | How to File for Divorce in NJ | $2 |
| | 1-57248-448-9 | How to Start a Business in NJ | $2 |

### NEW YORK TITLES

| Qty | ISBN | Title | R |
|---|---|---|---|
| | 1-57248-193-5 | Child Custody, Visitation and Support in NY | $2 |
| | 1-57248-351-2 | File for Divorce in NY | $2 |
| | 1-57248-249-4 | How to Form a Corporation in NY (2E) | $2 |
| | 1-57248-401-2 | How to Make a NY Will (3E) | $1 |
| | 1-57248-468-1 | How to Start a Business in NY (3E) | $2 |
| | 1-57248-198-6 | How to Win in Small Claims Court in NY (2E) | $1 |
| | 1-57248-122-6 | Tenants' Rights in NY | $2 |

### NORTH CAROLINA AND SOUTH CAROLINA TITLES

| Qty | ISBN | Title | R |
|---|---|---|---|
| | 1-57248-508-6 | How to File for Divorce in NC (4E) | $2 |
| | 1-57248-371-7 | How to Start a Business in NC or SC | $2 |
| | 1-57248-091-2 | Landlords' Rights & Duties in NC | $2 |

### OHIO TITLES

| Qty | ISBN | Title | R |
|---|---|---|---|
| | 1-57248-503-5 | How to File for Divorce in OH (3E) | $2 |
| | 1-57248-174-9 | How to Form a Corporation in OH | $2 |
| | 1-57248-173-0 | How to Make an OH Will | $1 |

### PENNSYLVANIA TITLES

| Qty | ISBN | Title | R |
|---|---|---|---|
| | 1-57248-242-7 | Child Custody, Visitation and Support in PA | $2 |
| | 1-57248-495-0 | How to File for Divorce in PA (4E) | $2 |
| | 1-57248-358-X | How to Form a Corporation in PA | $2 |
| | 1-57248-094-7 | How to Make a PA Will (2E) | $1 |
| | 1-57248-561-2 | Start a Business in PA (4E) | $2 |
| | 1-57248-245-1 | Landlords' Legal Guide in PA | $2 |

### TEXAS TITLES

| Qty | ISBN | Title | R |
|---|---|---|---|
| | 1-57248-171-4 | Child Custody, Visitation, and Support in TX | $2 |
| | 1-57248-541-8 | File for Divorce in TX (5E) | $2 |
| | 1-57248-470-5 | How to Form a Corporation in TX (3E) | $2 |
| | 1-57248-496-9 | How to Probate and Settle an Estate in TX (4E) | $2 |
| | 1-57248-471-3 | How to Start a Business in TX (4E) | $2 |
| | 1-57248-111-0 | How to Win in Small Claims Court in TX (2E) | $1 |
| | 1-57248-562-0 | Landlords' Legal Guide in TX (2E) | $2 |
| | 1-57248-513-2 | Write Your Own TX Will (4E) | $1 |

### WASHINGTON TITLES

| Qty | ISBN | Title | R |
|---|---|---|---|
| | 1-57248-522-1 | File for Divorce in WA | $2 |

SubTotal This page _____

SubTotal previous page _____

Shipping — $5.00 for 1st book, $1.00 each additional _____

Illinois residents add 6.75% sales tax _____

Connecticut residents add 6.00% sales tax _____

Total _____